HACKING WHISKEY

AARON GOLDFARB

HACKING
WHISKEY

Smoking, Blending, Fat Washing, and Other Whiskey Experiments

DOVETAIL

DOVETAIL

Text copyright © 2018 by Aaron Goldfarb
Photographs by Scott Gordon Bleicher
Illustrations by Carolyn Håkansson
Design by Justin Fuller
Prop styling by Christopher Spaulding

Published by Dovetail Press in Brooklyn, New York, a division of Assembly
Brands LLC.

For details or ordering information, contact the publisher at the address below
or email info@dovetail.press.

Dovetail Press
42 West Street #403
Brooklyn, NY 11222
www.dovetail.press

Library of Congress Cataloging-in-Publication data is on file with the publisher.

ISBN: 978-0-9996612-4-6

First printing, September 2018

Printed in China

10 9 8 7 6 5 4 3 2 1

Dedicated to Betsy, who married me and got 1,000 bottles of whiskey as well.

And Ellie, who has caused my camera roll to go from pictures of whiskeys I've drunk to ones of her. (Baby, don't try the following at home, please.)

CONTENTS

WHISK(E)Y DISCLAIMER
YOU HAVE TO INCLUDE TO PACIFY THE PEDANTS

—

In every whisk(e)y book published since Gutenberg, the poor author has to write a lame little note explaining exactly how he or she is going to spell whisk(e)y for the rest of the book. This is that note. For the rest of this book I will spell generic whiskey with an e. I will spell scotch and Japanese whisky without one. I will spell branded whiskey as the brand chooses to spell it. Maybe I'll screw up a few times. Maybe you'll go on Amazon and give me a one-star review because of that. Who cares? If you find yourself getting stressed out over how whiskey is spelled, have a whisky and relax.

RUN AWAY AND JOIN THE WHISKEY CIRCUS

In the summer of 2017, Buffalo Trace released its most audacious bourbon yet. From the same folks who infected the world with Pappymania came Old Rip Van Winkle 25 Year Old, the line's oldest ever expression. Only 710 bottles were made available—"allocated" is the parlance used in the industry—and they weren't even bottles per se. They were in handmade Glencairn Crystal decanters with silver toppers, packaged in a gorgeous wooden box (and I swear this isn't satire) constructed from the oak staves of the barrel that had once held the very bourbon. It also featured a certificate of authenticity, signed by Julian Van Winkle, suitable for framing perhaps, maybe in a frame also made from those oak staves.

All that for a retail cost of $1,800.

Although, if anyone on planet Earth actually paid that price, I never heard about it. Few bourbon drinkers ever even saw a bottle "in the wild." Instead, almost instantly, Old Rip Van Winkle 25 Year Old was selling on the online black market for $10,000-**plus.**

Julian Van Winkle, it should be noted, isn't the distiller of this prized whiskey and never has been. Julian Van Winkle doesn't even own a distillery. Julian Van Winkle is simply Pappy's grandson and the president of the Old Rip Van Winkle Distillery, now nothing more than a brand name owned by the Sazerac Company, whose Buffalo Trace *actually* distills all the Van Winkle products.

In reality, Julian Van Winkle could best be described as a P. T. Barnum–esque salesman par excellence. Over the last three decades, he has improbably turned the image of his grand-*pappy* (cough) smoking a stogie on bottles of, admittedly, pretty great bourbon (whose barrels he is said to hand-select) into a legend. The kind of legend folks clamor for. They chase liquor trucks to see where Pappy is headed and sleep overnight outside shops in the hopes of buying him first thing in the morning. They harass store employees about Pappy's whereabouts, enter lotteries in the hopes of winning him, and, sadly, have even started counterfeiting bottles of the old man. Such is the fervor that the Van Winkles will even sell ya a Pappy-branded T-shirt, golf visor, or end table if you really want it.

P. T. Barnum is an apt historical analogue for Julian Van Winkle, though, as whiskey today has become a total circus. Its multicolored big top is pitched over America, the land of baseball card collectors and Pokémon catchers, Beanie Baby snatchers and Comic-Conners, wine connoisseurs and cigar aficionados, and real estate flippers. You can now add whiskey hoarders to that list.

Question: Will any of the 710 people who landed Old Rip Van Winkle 25 Year Old actually drink it?

Better question: Would they even enjoy it if they did?

That's ultimately the craziest part of whiskey today. So many people are buying high-quality bourbons, rare ryes, ornate scotches, and exotic Japanese whiskies not to drink them, but simply to own them. To stockpile them in their "bunkers." To boast about their #whiskeyporn on Instagram. To maybe flip them for a profit to some other sucker who will start the same sad cycle all over again.

This book is not for those people. This book is for people who actually like whiskey. Who actually want to drink it.

Foundry Kitchen & Bar, a restaurant located in the Westin hotel in

YOU AIN'T GETTING ANY PAPPY

(ALTHOUGH IT'S NOT *QUITE* AS RARE AS YOU THINK)

PAPPY VAN WINKLE'S FAMILY RESERVE BOURBON	BOTTLES PRODUCED PER YEAR	RETAIL PRICE	BLACK MARKET PRICE
15 YEAR OLD	~16,000	$79.99	~$800
20 YEAR OLD	~12,000	$149.99	~$1,250
23 YEAR OLD	~8,000	$249.99	~$2,000

New York's Times Square, right across the street from Show World Center (once a 25-cent peep show), was one of 710 places to snag a bottle of Old Rip Van Winkle 25 Year Old. (They had, in fact, framed Julian Van Winkle's certificate and displayed it on the bar!) Now, while most New Yorkers wouldn't venture to Times Square for a drink even if there were a drought, plenty of others did.

The price they paid? $315 *an ounce.*

That's $315 to order a glass, Instagram it, down a sip or two, and maybe pair it with the restaurant's Times Square Cheeseburger. Then, if you actually want to catch a buzz, like the street urchins in *Oliver Twist*, ask: "Please, sir, may I have some more?" Yeah, for another $315, bucko!

Maybe you did that. Maybe you still want to. I'm here to tell you, you're better than that.

If you're not yet in the whiskey world and want to jump into the scene, it's probably too late. Too late to become a high-end collector, too late to acquire rare bottles, too late to possibly understand all the strange Willett bottlings and Four Roses barrel picks, certainly too late to find things like Pappy and Weller just sitting on store shelves. But that doesn't mean there isn't still fun to be had and plenty of whiskey to be drunk.

If you've already been in the whiskey world for a long time, maybe you're growing bored with the constant struggle to acquire "unicorn" bottles. You're surely growing broke from buying them on the secondary market (and sipping those $315 ounces). I know I am. It's time to start exploring another way. A better way.

You see, a lot of hobbyists are starting to do interesting things with their whiskey. Perhaps, like you, they have too many full bottles sitting on their man cave shelves. Maybe they have too much time on their hands. They could simply be bored. They almost certainly want to impress strangers online (but who doesn't?).

STOP CALLING IT "PAPPY"!

THESE ARE "PAPPY":
- Pappy Van Winkle's Family Reserve Bourbon 15 Year Old
- Pappy Van Winkle's Family Reserve Bourbon 20 Year Old
- Pappy Van Winkle's Family Reserve Bourbon 23 Year Old

LET'S BE BLUNT. THE FOLLOWING ARE *NOT* "PAPPY," (AND YOU SOUND LIKE AN IDIOT WHEN YOU CALL THEM "PAPPY"):
- Old Rip Van Winkle 10 Year Old (this is *not* "Pappy 10"!)
- Van Winkle Special Reserve 12 Year "Lot B" (this is *not* "Pappy 12"!)
- Old Rip Van Winkle 25 Year Old (this is *not* "Pappy 25"!)
- Van Winkle Family Reserve Rye (this is *not* "Pappy Rye"!)

I am just one man reporting from the field. One man who spends far too much time in bars and distilleries and even strangers' homes, but, more often, on Reddit, Instagram, private Facebook groups, and other odd factions of the Internet. I love seeing how people are playing with their whiskey these days.

There are DIYers who have begun blending whiskey at home. Like Blake Riber, who, when frustrated by the tricky task of finding Pappy Van Winkle, figured out an ersatz blend he dubbed "Poor Man's Pappy." (Although, crazily enough, even Poor Man's Pappy has become hard to create these days. Which is why I'll also teach you about "Poorer Man's Pappy.") There's Danny Strongwater, whose amateur "California Gold" blend is so good it, too, became an unexpected hit on the secondary market. Other folks have started pet projects for the most outrageous blend of them all, the infinity bottle.

There are drinkers who, wanting to gild the lily, have begun "finishing" commercial whiskeys with other spirits like port, sherry, and cognac (you'll need a tiny barrel for this). Armagnac-finished George T. Stagg? Yes, please. We'll look into the realm of even crazier experimentation, more of the culinary type, like smoking whiskey to add new flavors and "fat washing" to infuse it with everything from bacon to buttered blue corn to foie gras to even Butterfingers and Heath bars. (Yes, step-by-step instructions and recipes will be included.)

Finally, you're going to learn how to waste your whiskey. Yes, *waste* it, instead of treating it like a precious elixir, never to be opened. In the final chapter you'll see how to "whiskey-age" your steak and how to do a bone-marrow luge. We'll meet a Louisville bar owner who once made $10 Pappy Jell-O shots (take that, Foundry!). We'll hear about acclaimed chef Sean Brock, who produced Pappy 23 vinegar—yes, literally turning America's most coveted bourbon *nonalcoholic*. You can even make your whiskey into soap if you like, and bathe in its splendor. How's that for spectacular wastefulness?

But, first, we need to stock the house.

CHAPTER 1

STOCKING
THE HOUSE

WHISKEY STONES ARE STUPID (ALCOHOL ADULTERATORS YOU COULD TRULY USE)

Holidays and birthdays are always tough when friends and family members know you as a "whiskey lover." Not confident enough to buy you a bottle, not generous enough to spring for something unquestionably nice, they instead get you a whiskey tchotchke. (They also think you're an alcoholic, perhaps another reason for skipping the bottle-as-gift.) And what's front and center in the whiskey tchotchke aisle? You guessed it, whiskey stones.

I could fill a fishbowl with all the stupid whiskey stones I've been gifted over the years. But I'll tell ya, I don't know a single whiskey lover who actually uses these things. Chilling whiskey has never been an all-too-difficult endeavor. Ice works just fine. And most of us like our whiskey neat anyhow because, you know, we all like to *taste* the whiskey.

Even worse are moonshine-aging kits, which are rarely cheap. As anyone ever gifted one has quickly learned, putting eyeglass cleaner-quality white dog in a tiny-ass barrel won't ever produce something better than even bottom-shelf, plastic-handle bourbon—whether you age it for an hour or a decade. But the thought of meddling with whiskey at home is still a good one, and having a tiny barrel on your desk is undoubtedly cool.

There are better ways to play with whiskey. More fun methods of alcohol adulteration. Ones that actually produce a product worthy of drinking—not to mention ones that are truly unique, never to be created by any multimillion-dollar distillery.

And you won't even have to spend much money to acquire everything you need to stock the house and get started.

BUYING GREAT WHISKEY WHEN YOU HAVE NO CONNECTIONS AND/OR ARE BROKE

Honestly, sometimes it seems like it might be cheaper to collect classic Porsches than whiskey. It can be depressing to see certain acclaimed bottles on the shelves, or high-end bar menus, and calculate that enough drams to get you buzzed might cost more than a week's worth of groceries. What's a whiskey lover to do? Well, a few things.

SEE THE BEAUTY IN UGLY BOTTLES

While it's easy to look at a bottle boxed in oak staves or swathed in luxurious velvet and presume it houses something delicious, the inverse also kinda feels true. Surely that bottom-shelf bottle with the shoddy label and plastic  twist cap can't be tasty? *Wrong.* Many so-called "cheap" whiskeys, like Wild Turkey 101 and Rittenhouse Rye, are terrific products and a great place for an aspiring connoisseur to start. Old Grand-Dad Bonded is made from the same "juice" as the much costlier and more fancily packaged Basil Hayden's—and OGD is higher proof!

YOU DOWN WITH MGP?

By now even your teetotaling mom knows that a lot of micro-whiskey isn't legit, but instead comes sourced from a giant Indiana factory named MGP

(Midwest Grain Products) Ingredients. The thing is, though, many MGP whiskeys are damn good, especially their 95% ryes, which have an utterly distinct note (some say of pickle juice). Many of the more famed "craft" distilleries—High West, Smooth Ambler—use at least a portion of MGP liquid in their whiskeys, and, while those products are terrific and well-priced, many other (more secretive) MGP sourcers are way overcharging you for the privilege. If you like the MGP flavor profile, grab some bottles of Bulleit Rye, James E. Pepper, and George Dickel Rye Whisky, which are made from MGP juice but can typically be found a whole lot cheaper than other, more "crafty" MGP employers like Angel's Envy and WhistlePig.

LOOK TO THE IRISH

Bourbon and rye are red hot, scotch has always been pricey, and any Japanese whisky of note is becoming impossible to find in America. That leaves us with the Irish, who have as lengthy a whiskey history as the Scottish but for some reason are unable to sell their better products for the same astronomical amounts. That's silly, as there are plenty of phenomenal Irish whiskeys that are as delicious as anything else out there. I always recommend Redbreast 12 Year Old ($55) as a great, affordable gift, and Powers John's Lane as another underpriced winner. (And quality Canadian whisky, like J.P. Wiser's and Lot No. 40, is even cheaper.)

LOVE THE BARREL-PROOF

Booker's isn't just tasty; it's also around 125 proof. More bang for your buck! Even if whiskey connoisseurship isn't (completely) about getting blotto, man can only drink so much whiskey in a single night. Maybe that's a whole bottle of Jack per day if you're Lemmy from Motörhead (RIP); maybe only a few ounces if you're a normal person without a liver made of titanium and an ability to blast power chords on your bass. So you better make those drams count, and, if you're broke, you better get as much out of your bottle as you can. Thus, your best bet is to go after "barrel-proof" offerings, i.e., whiskey that hasn't been watered down whatsoever.

Most important for this book's sake: higher-proof whiskeys are better at accomplishing what we are trying to do in the following pages— injecting and infusing additional flavors into commercial whiskey. Alcohol is an astringent, so the higher the proof, the better the product is at grabbing flavors from a barrel, another spirit, or some foodstuff.

SOME RECOMMENDED BOTTLES THAT ARE STILL EASY TO FIND AND STILL A GOOD VALUE

- Wild Turkey 101 (rye and bourbon)
- Old Grand-Dad Bonded and 114
- Old Overholt
- Rittenhouse Rye
- Elijah Craig Small Batch
- Evan Williams Single Barrel
- Wild Turkey Rare Breed (barrel proof)
- Booker's Vintage (barrel proof)
- Stagg Jr. (barrel proof)

ON "DUSTY HUNTING"

Search the hashtag #dustyhunting on Instagram and . . . well, you'll see a bunch of weirdo nail polish collectors excited to have found an old bottle of Sally Hansen Pacific Blue Original Formula. We're talking about another kind of weirdo here, however—whiskey collectors who look for old bottles of high-

quality "juice" hiding in plain sight. Unfortunately, "dusty hunting," as it's called, is pretty much over. I used to know dudes who would dedicate entire weekends to driving in concentric circles around a certain part of town—usually the cruddier part of town, like where Eminem grew up—hitting hundreds of liquor stores, hoping to find some ancient bottle of Old Fitzgerald still lingering on a shelf, covered in dust. It was a great way back then to grab something totally killer for pennies.

Even just a year or two ago, you could occasionally stumble upon a 1960s Weller or out-of-production Wild Turkey age-stated bottling. Those days are all but over. Your better option is to finally accept your grandpa or great aunt's long-standing invitation to come over for Sunday pot roast. After the soup course, sneak off to the wet bar, and maybe you'll find some old whiskey untouched since it was last actually drunk back in the '80s. As for me, when my grandpa died a couple years back, the best thing I found in his liquor cabinet was a sticky bottle of neon-green Midori.

BUYING AN ENTIRE BARREL (LIKE A BOSS)

If owning a lot of bottles of whiskey is cool, you know what's really cool? Owning an entire barrel.

Yes, many American whiskey distilleries today are letting your favorite bars, restaurants, liquor stores, supermarkets, and the like handpick one-of-a-kind barrels of their bourbons and ryes. These can be sold to customers, used to make special "house" cocktails, or even given away as gifts.

More savvy whiskey consumers are purchasing entire barrels for themselves too.

What exactly does "buying a barrel" actually mean? No, I'm sorry to say, you won't get the full, 500-pound barrel delivered to your front door, no matter how sweet that may sound. (Kegger!) Instead, with around 53 gallons of liquid per barrel, and accounting for loss from the so-called angel's share and other acts of "spillage," one barrel at cask-strength will eventually yield around 150 standard 750-milliliter bottles.

In the case of many of the Kentucky and Tennessee distilleries, if you're interested in owning a barrel's worth of booze, you simply schedule a visit, get yourself down to, say, Lawrenceburg or Frankfort, and then take a tasting tour, sometimes sipping directly from various barrels. Since single barrels will naturally vary in both flavor profile and ABV (alcohol by volume) due to how and where they've been aged, the exact same theoretical expressions from any given company can taste completely different. One smoky, one fruity, one viscous and caramely, the other thinner and vanilla laced. Find one you like and you can buy a barrel on the spot, just like Dad might've picked out his new Buick. Only this car will take a month or two to get delivered to you. It'll come with personalized tags to boot—just like a vanity plate.

The only rub? You'll need a liquor license. Or an acquaintance with one who's willing to make the purchase on your behalf (of course many liquor stores are more than happy to immediately buy $10,000 worth of booze in one shot for a

customer . . . even if they've never met you before). You're neither getting ripped off nor getting a bulk discount, unfortunately—the barrel costs the same exact price as it would cost to purchase the equivalent number of bottles.

And, yes, you do get to keep that empty barrel as well. If your wife will let you. Now you just need to figure out what to do with it (or you could peek ahead to The Barrel Refill Project on page 62).

A FEW DISTILLERIES
OFFERING BARREL "PICKS"

(for contact info, see Resources on page 256)

- Barrell Bourbon
- Dad's Hat Pennsylvania Rye Whiskey (offering Single Barrel Cask Strength Rye)
- Four Roses (Private Selection Barrel Proof)
- High West (many one-of-a-kind barrels)
- Jack Daniel's (Single Barrel Select)
- Jim Beam (Knob Creek)
- Maker's Mark (Maker's Mark Cask Strength, which can be customized with a bespoke stave arrangement)
- Old Forester (Single Barrel)
- Sazerac (Buffalo Trace, Eagle Rare, Blanton's, and Old Weller Antique)
- WhistlePig (Single Barrel Select 10 Year)
- Wild Turkey (Russell's Reserve Single Barrel Bourbon and Kentucky Spirit)
- Woodford Reserve (Distiller's Select Personal Selection, Double Oaked Single Barrel By the Barrel)
- Wyoming Whiskey (Private Stock)

MAJOR ITEMS YOU'LL NEED FOR YOUR "TOY BOX"

Now that you have a decent whiskey selection, if not an entire barrel, it's time to acquire the tools to adulterate it. While some of the recipes in the following pages will ask for singular items you might never need again, these tools will be called for again and again. With just the following in your home, you can produce the vast majority of the book's recipes.

BASIC BAR TOOLS

A jigger, shaker, mixing glass, strainer, bar spoon, and muddler should do. A funnel, graduated cylinder, and eye-dropper all the better.

A TINY BARREL

A 1- or 2-liter size should do—any larger and you won't be able to afford to fill it. If part of a moonshine-aging kit, ditch the moonshine or use it to remove some Pacific Blue Original Formula nail polish. Many online retailers today sell tiny barrels, for less than $100 in most cases. Sometimes you can even get something burned into the head of the barrel, like your name or that silly logo for the fake bar you own that you once designed on a cocktail napkin. The Oak Bottle, a literal bottle made of wood, is also terrific for aging in small amounts. I like to use that for my test batches.

DECANTER

Not an absolute necessity, although always good for making you look like a well-heeled southern senator. Try to find one without lead in it (see page 70).

EMPTY BOTTLES

Repurposed bottles from whiskeys you've finished are completely fine. Better are 375-milliliter bottles purchased from online retailers like Amazon.

CHEESECLOTH

A standard pack of culinary cheesecloths, which you can grab in most supermarkets for cheap. I guarantee you'll forget to buy some and end up needing to use a dish rag or a few coffee filters instead. Those'll work too. And a chinois strainer will work even better, though it's tougher to pronounce when asking the salesman to direct you to the correct store aisle.

CULINARY TORCH

Oh, yeah, we'll be lighting shit on fire.

SMOKING GUN PRO

Disable the detectors and open some windows—this is a powerful tool.

COURAGE (OPTIONAL)

You will be taking whiskey that is already delicious and for which you paid your hard-earned money . . . and potentially rendering it awful. Balls, my friend, balls. Drink some whiskey to get there if need be.

SOCIAL MEDIA ACCOUNTS TO BRAG ON (OPTIONAL)

If the world doesn't know you did something awesome, what's the point?

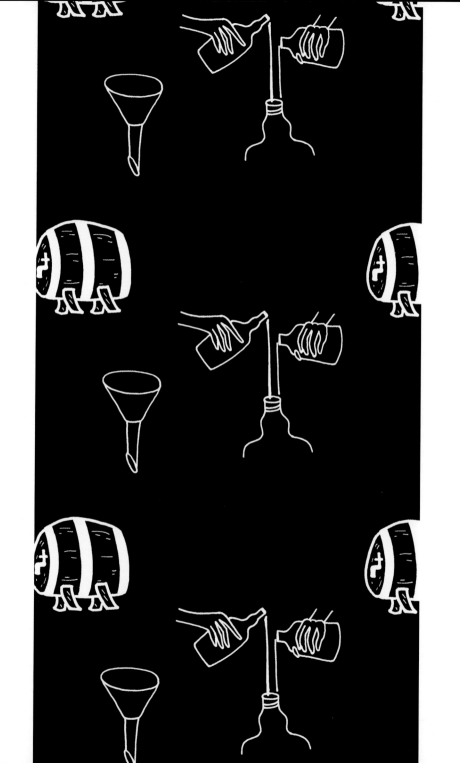

CHAPTER 2

BLENDING

VATTING
IS WHERE IT'S AT

California Gold. The late fall of 2016 was the first time I heard the name. I was at a private whiskey tasting up in New Hampshire. The owner of the house is a friend and has all the bottles you want to try but perhaps have never even seen before. Van Winkles. George T. Staggs and Thomas H. Handys. Four Roses limited editions. That sorta stuff. Because of my friend, I've been lucky enough to try all these "unicorn" bottles, and, thus, they don't hold a ton of interest for me anymore. They're great, sure, but I'm more concerned about finding the hot new thing. Which

means, what did catch my attention on that chilly November day, was this one bottle I'd never seen before.

It looked like a joke. Something a child had designed. It was squat, a 375-milliliter round bottle with a white HP LaserJet label sloppily affixed to it. On the label were blurry clip-art images of what I'd later learn was "crap off the Internet pasted together" by West Coast whiskey enthusiast Danny Strongwater (not his real name). An avid collector of high-end whiskey, he wanted to see if he could blend together other legitimate whiskeys into his own perfect blend. A lover of older Willett Family Estate bottlings—which have become scarce and quite costly on the secondary market—Strongwater wanted to attempt to make something similarly complex yet more accessible and obviously cheaper.

Sounds silly, but upon trying California Gold that first time, I was blown away. It was better than anything else I had tried or would try that day.

"What's in this?!" I eagerly asked my friend.

"No one knows, and he won't tell."

By this point, California Gold was already an underground sensation, trading avidly through secret online whiskey forums. Strongwater would make a batch of a dozen bottles or so and distribute them among the whiskey community. By the time I became familiar with him, he was up to around his twentieth batch or so, one he simply called "California Gold: XXX".

It's not just Strongwater, though. When I first wrote about California Gold for PUNCH—a top drinks website—in March of 2017, many in-the-know enthusiasts agreed with my praise. California Gold was *that* good. Other commenters pooh-poohed me, claiming they "make a much better blend." So I decided to solicit some of these cocky amateurs for their own "vatting" recipes; many were indeed outstanding. I've likewise humbly created a few blends myself, which will also be included in the following pages.

DAVID PERKINS

—

A former biochemist, Perkins was inspired by the science inherent in fermentation and distilling to move to Park City, Utah, and open his own distillery, High West, in 2007, starting in a small downtown location. Mostly sourcing whiskey from places like MGP and Barton early on, Perkins had to quickly become a master of blending if he was to differentiate his products. He would soon find success with such blends as Bourye, a bourbon/rye combination, and Campfire, the world's first blend of peated scotch and American whiskeys. In 2016 High West was sold to Constellation Brands for $160 million; a few months later it was named *Whisky Advocate's* Distiller of the Year. In his own words on the subject of blending . . .

The whole whiskey thing came up on me fast. I was happily employed at a biotech company when I went to a wedding in Kentucky where, on a whim, I took a Maker's Mark tour. I had started life as a chemist, and you walk through a distillery and it's all chemistry. I looked around Maker's and told Jane, my wife, "Shoot, we oughta make some whiskey."

It's hard to start a business just distilling your own product, though. It was Jim Rutledge from Four Roses who told me it would make more sense to start by outsourcing whiskey. We knew everyone was buying MGP's 95% rye. But I wanted to create my own blends because I didn't want to sell the same outsourced product that everyone else was selling. It was a way to competitively differentiate ourselves. And hopefully make something that tasted better.

We learned blending from the Seagram's guys. They never intended that 95% rye to be drunk on its own. It was always for adding a sharp rye note to blends in order to create a pleasant profile. Selling it on its own was a unique concept. So it's not that blending itself was super unique. We were just the first place to actually talk about our blends.

We would always buy big lots of stuff when they would come up for sale. We can use that here; we can use that there. For instance, once we bought a big lot of bourbon from a Lawrenceburg, Kentucky, distillery that wouldn't let us use their name. But we thought we could find some way to blend it. Maybe get some other stocks to mix with it to create something special. Eventually that became our American Prairie.

We once had a two-year-old rye that was kinda hot, but also tasted pretty good. It was certainly different. Then we also had a 16-year-old rye. To be honest, it was way too woody. You wouldn't want to sell either of those on their own. But together, the woody 16-year-old calmed down when added to the semihot two-year-old. The whiskey components by themselves, yeah, you'd drink 'em apart, but it was certainly much better to drink them blended together. That's how we created Double Rye!

I learned about blending older whiskey into younger whiskey from the master distiller at Seagram's, Larry Ebersold. When Pernod Ricard bought them in 2000 he was cleaning up some Wild Turkey stock they had in a warehouse, as they owned them as well at the time. I told him I loved their 1990s-era Russell's Reserve 10 Year Old. He told me that's because it probably had a lot of much older, more woody bourbon blended into it and 10 years was just the *youngest* component.

You don't know what will work 'til you try it. At High West, we generally start by sampling what's in the warehouse. We're tasting individual glasses from different barrels. After you get very good at it, it's just like cooking. A really good chef, he can just throw things together or take leftovers and mix them together and it'll work. Because they aren't starting from scratch. They already know the flavor profiles of everything they have. It's the same for whiskey blenders. Some can just create mixes in their heads.

At the end of the day, though, blending is just combining things you think would go well together and tasting them. Your instincts will guide you. Combine one part of this with four parts of that. Then keep tweaking until you get something you're really happy with.

Always let a blend sit in the bottle over the weekend. We wouldn't even do taste experiments if a blend hadn't had time to sit for a couple of days. Of course, now, once we get a recipe down, we can immediately just mix it. Because once it goes into bottles there's plenty of time for it to sit in warehouses waiting to be shipped out.

Campfire took six months to get the recipe right. The smoke component would keep changing in the bottle after a couple of days. Peated whiskey doesn't take much for you to really taste it. Just an extra 1% has a really big impact. At least it did for us. We didn't think we'd ever get it right. Part of it was finding, not the right scotch, but the right bourbon. We eventually ended up adding some rye, too, to really make it pop. It was also finding the right scotch of course. We were buying bottles of commercially-available scotches. Ones with different levels of peat. It took us six months and 80 different blends to get the components and the proportions right. Then we had to see if we could source it on a larger scale.

For our first A Midwinter Night's Dram, we had 15 different samples of Rendezvous Rye, different barrels with different finishes in different glasses. We were sitting around a table "speed-dating" those, trying them all. I tasted two of them. Oh, these are really good. One was aged in port barrels; one aged in a new French oak. Gosh, these both taste Christmasy, I thought. What if we mixed them together? So I mixed this fruity, cherry port-finished one with this clovy, woody French oak-finished one . . . voilà!

That was an idea in my head that instantly came to life. Then we just had to scale it up.

We screw up plenty of blends of course. One year, a guy forgot to taste a few barrels that were going to make Midwinter. So we just went ahead and blended it—five barrels of the port-aged, six barrels of the French oak. Two thousand gallons or so. We just mixed the whole thing together. And it tasted bad. Very bad. One barrel had been musty and ruined the entire batch. We had to toss it. A sad, sad day.

Today blending is an easy way for distilleries to set themselves apart. Our blend is "proprietary," they'll say. Maybe it is; maybe it isn't. It's different, though, and it's a lot easier to be different that way. As opposed to actually making good whiskey, which is still very hard to do.

HOW TO BLEND IN

Danny Strongwater thinks that what California Gold proves most of all is that the big Kentucky distilleries should be collaborating more often, in the same way craft breweries do. He feels if they blended together their different products made with unique house yeast strains, mash bills, flavor profiles, and "funk," they could create truly extraordinary products, greater than the sum of their parts. Until then, though, he'll keep doing it himself: "It's like blending wine. If you have a barrel of Syrah that's not sweet enough, well, I have another one that is just the opposite."

While there's no right or wrong way when it comes to blending, the following is a good template to help you get started.

1. Figure out the overall flavor profile you're going for. Do you want a particularly syrupy and sweet bourbon to have some peppery or smoky notes in the background? Dream big!

2. Look for commercially made whiskeys that have high amounts of the flavor notes you want to include. Perhaps even unbalanced notes if you were to sip it alone.

3. Start experimenting, first building blends in very small amounts, 2 ounces total for instance. Measure precisely and write down the statistics of each  blend so you can scale from miniature to full size if and once you finally nail a recipe. Strongwater claims as little as 5 milliliters (about $\frac{1}{5}$ ounce) of something can make a massive difference in a 750-milliliter bottle. He insists too many people think they need a 60/40- or 60/20/20-type blend.

4. If you think you've found a blend you like, allow it to sit for a few days to let the ingredients marry.

5. Controversially, Strongwater claims it's crucial to shake the bottle to integrate the blend and also release all the "barrel char" flavor. Many online commenters think that's downright hooey. Whatever the case, it isn't much effort to take him at his word.

6. Once you've found a blend you like, scale it up. And change the world!

• •

On the following pages are a few recommended blends to help you get the hang of it. Blends are rendered via percentages of components, to allow you to produce them at whatever volume you wish.

DANNY STRONGWATER'S

CALIFORNIA GOLD

Strongwater famously won't reveal exactly what's in his blend. In fact, the only other person who knows is his partner; he's instructed her to pass it on to a friend of his should he die. Despite such secrecy, Strongwater has offered the community a few hints. He's implied that the base is a barrel-proof Buffalo Trace product with strong oak character—most believe that to be Stagg Jr. Others think the spice comes from a Four Roses Single Barrel. Some naysayers claim Strongwater uses sherry and even añejo tequila for some of the more complex notes—it seems possible, but that doesn't make me admire California Gold any less. Strongwater has also told me one of the components is not readily available anymore, and thus California Gold's days may be numbered.

51%+ STAGG JR.

??% FOUR ROSES SINGLE BARREL

??% SHERRY

??% AÑEJO TEQUILA

??% ???

GOLD FLAKES (OPTIONAL)

Although guessing Strongwater's exact blend is virtually impossible, a decent analogue I've been able to put together is 65% Stagg Jr., 20% Four Roses Single Barrel OBSQ (for the floral, herbal notes), 10% Booker's (for a hint of peanut), and 5% PX sherry.

OLD COUSIN TOUCHERS

After the viral success of my California Gold article, I started getting a lot of taunting messages from people who claimed they had, or certainly knew of, a much better home blend. One kept coming up: Old Cousin Touchers.

I couldn't tell if this was something real or if online trolls were merely messing with me courtesy of some inside joke (the online bourbon world has *tons* of trolling jokes). Eventually, though, I located a grainy image of OCT's homemade label, two youthful hands reaching out to each other à la Michelangelo's *The Creation of Adam*. Nevertheless, Google brought up virtually no information on this supposed "Family Reserve" blend. Determined to figure out if it truly existed, after several months of searching, I finally found its creator (who asked to remain anonymous).

In 2012 he was a bartender at famed whiskey den Delilah's Chicago and was getting sick of coming home after work and (accidentally) opening great bottles at 4:00 a.m. "It was really depressing the next day," he told me. "Man, I opened *that* up? I killed *that*?" Thus he came up with an ingenious plan: He would build a blend from readily available bourbons that would still appease his late-night palate as if he were drinking something old and rare.

He was inspired by the Poor Man's Pappy (then known as the Weller Centennial Tribute) blend that had first appeared on

Straightbourbon, a bourbon-centric website, and likewise wanted to create an all-wheated blend.

"I was mimicking the Van Winkle approach before Buffalo Trace was distilling Pappy. Back then Julian was taking wheated bourbon from three different places and blending to taste," he explained. "Luckily, there are lots of super-decent wheated options to work with these days."

As for the name, it's a play on all the cheap but pretty solid-tasting "Olds" of yesteryear, most notably Old Commonwealth, a private-label bourbon bottled by Julian Van Winkle, that the bartenders at Delilah's enjoyed shooting during their shifts. The bartenders liked to joke that one day they would create their own cheap bourbon called Old Cousin Touchers—a bluntly off-color joke about, yes, Kentucky and inbreeding. A friend designed the initial label for the so-called Crooked Kentucky Bourbon, which is supposed to be reminiscent of an Old Fitzgerald Bottled-in-Bond label that is still used by OCT to this very day. One big batch is blended every year, usually around the holidays, with a few given out as gifts. Some are even said to be residing, hidden of course, behind the bars in Chicago and beyond.

In this recipe, as Old Weller Antique Single Barrel and Larceny both have widely varying flavor profiles, Maker's Mark Cask Strength is used at the end, to taste, to arrive at the correct "beefiness" and sweetness. The final proof should be around 100.

50% LARCENY

50% OLD WELLER ANTIQUE 107 (SINGLE BARREL SELECT)

MAKER'S MARK CASK STRENGTH, TO TASTE

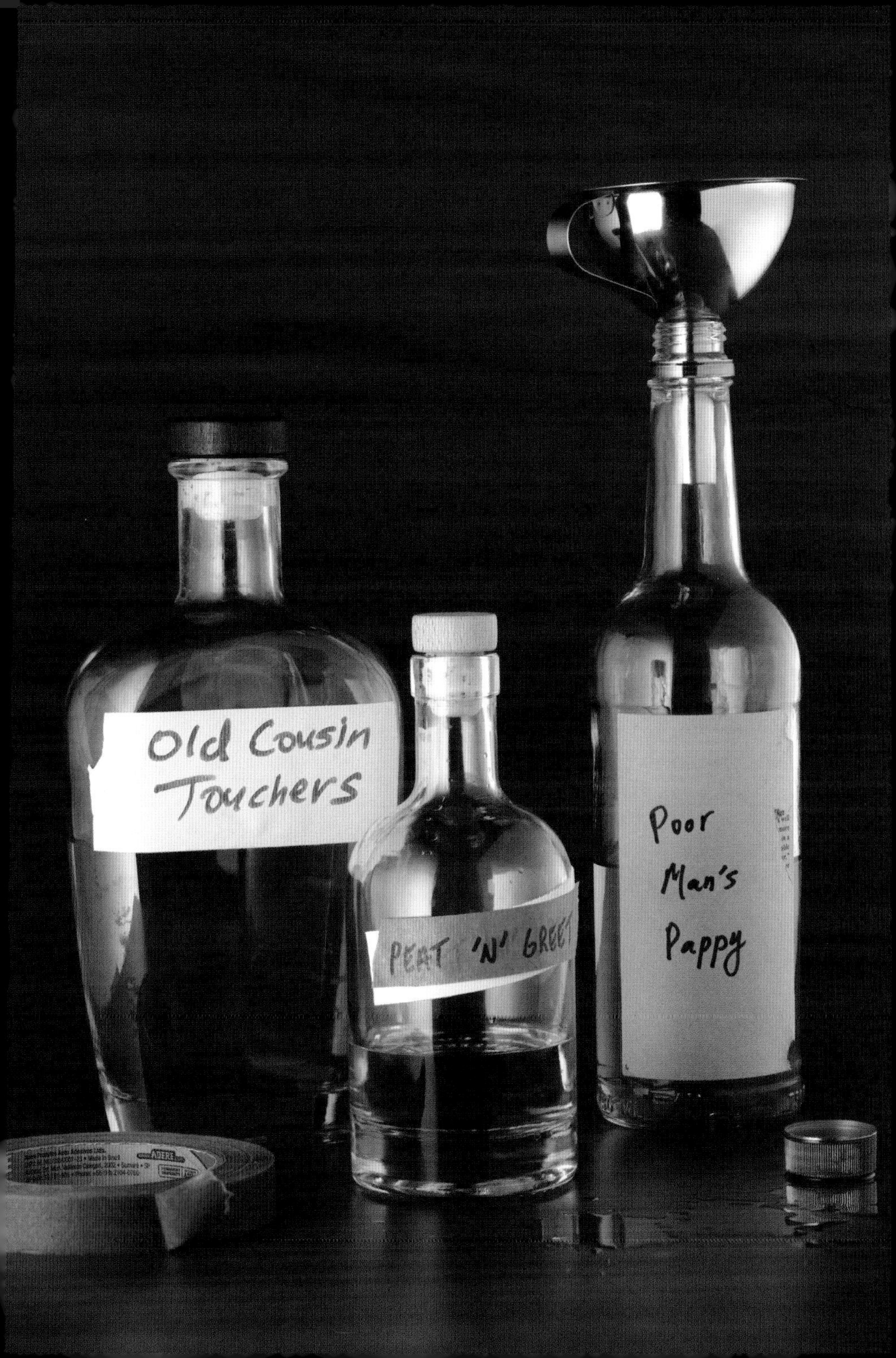
Old Cousin Touchers
PEAT 'N' GREET
Poor Man's Pappy

BLAKE RIBER'S

POOR MAN'S PAPPY

While many still dispute who first coined the term—are you starting to realize whiskey nerds argue a lot?—a man named Blake Riber is generally credited with inventing the so-called "Poor Man's Pappy." ("I tell people I created the name but not the blend. I stole the blend from forums on Straightbourbon," he told me, to be fair.) Riber, the author of the popular whiskey blog Bourbonr, first discussed his blend in late 2013. Tired of scouring stores for Pappy Van Winkle bottles, and refusing to pay huge black-market rates, Riber decided to genetically engineer a Franken-Winkle. Knowing that Pappy is a wheated mash bill from Buffalo Trace, Riber figured he could mix cheaper Buffalo Trace "wheaters" to eventually find the perfect blend. Although the combined blend totals only 100.2 proof, many believe it tastes somewhat similar to Pappy Van Winkle 15 Year Old. (Some folks like to add an oak stick to the vat to improve barrel character.)

60% OLD WELLER ANTIQUE 107

40% W.L. WELLER 12 YEAR

POORER MAN'S PAPPY

Don't get too excited, though. Thanks to the proliferation of chatter about Poor Man's Pappy—and goons learning that Weller products are kinda sorta "the pappiez"—bottles of Old Weller Antique, and, especially Weller 12, are now almost as hard to find as the Van Winkles. Once you could find these Wellers easily for around $25 . . . now they, too, elicit camping out at stores and entering lotteries. Sad. Thus, I decided to see if I could make a *Poorer* Man's Pappy, using some wheated bourbons that are actually findable these days. Maker's Mark is a good choice as it is said Pappy helped Bill Samuels Sr. develop his original wheated recipe and process. Using Maker's Mark Cask Strength—with bottlings typically in the 108- to 114-proof range—then calming it down with some Larceny, allows us to hit the 107-proof of Pappy 15 right on the nose. Of course, I'm sure by the time you're reading this book we'll need a Poorest Man's Pappy. Or, we could all just try drinking something else.

67% MAKER'S MARK CASK STRENGTH

33% LARCENY

DAVID JENNINGS'S

KENTUCK-EH

Jennings is the Internet's preeminent Wild Turkey fan, always on the lookout for interesting releases from over the years. He also enjoys playing with firewater at his home in South Carolina. "I like blending different rye whiskeys together," he told me. "I seem to have better luck with that over bourbon." Naturally, his favorite home blend employs Wild Turkey rye, which he combines with Vermont's WhistlePig, which sources some of its rye barrels from Alberta, Canada. As for the name, he bluntly explains, "Yes, that's a Canuck joke."

As the Russell's Reserve is a more corn-heavy, "barely legal" rye, it beautifully complements WhistlePig's highly herbaceous, floral notes.

60% RUSSELL'S RESERVE SINGLE BARREL RYE

40% WHISTLEPIG 10 YEAR SINGLE BARREL (CASK STRENGTH)

WE WANT THE FUNK

Jennings is most obsessed with dusty Wild Turkey, which many connoisseurs claim has a unique, almost indescribable "funk." Seen in now-discontinued bottles with silly nicknames like Split Label (1993), Pewter Top (1994), Donut (1998), and, most amusingly, Cheesy Gold Foil (1985 to 1992), these Wild Turkey expressions are extremely oily on the mouthfeel, perfume-like on the nose, with a flavor profile bouncing between leather, pipe tobacco, cellar mustiness, and even blue cheese. They've also become increasingly rare, and thus quite pricey on the black market. You're looking at $500+ a bottle. Unfortunately, today's modern Wild Turkey expressions, while quite good, don't have that "funk" for whatever reason (speculation cites everything from a change in yeasts to the 1989 removal of cancer-causing urethane to even crumbling cork stoppers creating oxidation). Still, if you're a humble whiskey fan who wants to try the funk for yourself, and doesn't have the money or connections to land an old bottle, Jennings recommends this blend of newer stuff. It won't be that cheap, however, owing to the Master's Keep, but it will be funky and a solid stand-in.

65% RUSSELL'S RESERVE SINGLE BARREL BOURBON

35% WILD TURKEY MASTER'S KEEP

BEAM SUNTORY

In this age where good ol' *'Murican* brands are being commandeered by international conglomerates, I wanted to see if I could synergize a few blends from the same portfolio but from different countries. Beam Suntory is a good place to start. In 2014 Suntory Holdings purchased Beam Inc. for around $16 billion, creating perhaps the most wide-ranging whiskey portfolio in the entire world. On the American side, it now owned all of Jim Beam's great products, which extend to Maker's Mark, Old Grand-Dad, and small-batch stuff like Knob Creek and Booker's. On the Japanese side, it has the powerhouses Yamazaki, Hakushu, and Hibiki.

Let this blend sit in the gorgeous Harmony bottle. Of course, Beam Suntory also owns great scotch, namely the Islay peat bombs coming out of Laphroaig and Bowmore. Add a "floater" of either (5%) if you'd like to introduce some smoke.

40% HIBIKI JAPANESE HARMONY

35% JIM BEAM DEVIL'S CUT

15% SUNTORY WHISKY TOKI

10% BASIL HAYDEN'S

OTHER CONGLOMERATE BLENDS TO TRY

THE DIAGEO

55% Johnnie Walker Black Label

30% Bulleit Rye

10% Lagavulin 16 Year Old

5% Crown Royal Maple

THE PERNOD RICARD

50% Powers Irish Whiskey

40% The Glenlivet 12 Year Old

10% Smooth Ambler Contradiction

THE CONSTELLATION

60% High West Rendezvous Rye

35% Black Velvet Whisky

5% Black Velvet Cinnamon Rush

THE MOËT HENNESSY

65% Glenmorangie The Original

25% Woodinville Straight American Whiskey

10% Ardbeg Uigeadail

WILLIAM GRANT & SONS

55% Glenfiddich Bourbon Barrel Reserve 14 Year Old

34% The Balvenie Doublewood 12

10% Tullamore D.E.W. Original

1% Hudson Baby Bourbon

MULTIGRAIN

While all bourbon is made mostly of corn (it has to be), it usually also includes a touch of barley and then either rye or wheat. Of late, distilleries have started using more than three grains per mash bill and sometimes even strange, atypical grains like oats, millet, and triticale. Colonel E. H. Taylor released a product called Four Grain in 2017 that instantly became a darling on the secondary market. I decided I wanted to blow them away with my multigrain blend, which counts 10 different grains in its recipe (barley, wheat, rye, triticale, corn, buckwheat, rice, sorghum, oat, and millet . . . *phew!*).

Try your hand at this fancy-ass concoction, then convince some geek on the Internet to Venmo you $1,000 for the rare bottle.

30% WESTLAND AMERICAN SINGLE MALT WHISKEY

20% MAKER'S 46

15% DAD'S HAT PENNSYLVANIA RYE WHISKEY

7% DRY FLY STRAIGHT TRITICALE WHISKEY

7% MELLOW CORN

5% CORSAIR BUCK YEAH

5% KIKORI WHISKEY

5% NEW SOUTHERN REVIVAL SORGHUM WHISKEY

3% HIGH WEST SILVER WESTERN OAT

3% KOVAL MILLET

BOB CARON'S

MULTI-NATIONAL MULTI-GRAIN WEDDING BLEND

Surely the most insane, I mean *ambitious*, blend I've seen online comes from the excellent WHISKEY VATTING private Facebook group. This spicy, rye-heavy blend combines multiple grains from five different whiskey-producing countries: Scotland, Ireland, France, Canada, and the United States. The New England man posted that he made this for his nephew's wedding, claiming the bottle was easily finished off that very night.

28% CANADIAN CLUB CLASSIC 12 YEAR OLD

14% J.P. WISER'S LEGACY CANADIAN WHISKY

11% KNAPPOGUE CASTLE 14 YEAR OLD

11% LOT NO. 40 CANADIAN WHISKY

11% GLEN MASTER 11 YEAR OLD (SPRINGBANK)

8% BRENNE FRENCH SINGLE MALT WHISKY

5.5% HIGH WEST RENDEZVOUS RYE

5.5% KNOB CREEK STRAIGHT RYE WHISKEY

3% HIGHLAND PARK 12 YEAR OLD VIKING HONOUR

3% WILD TURKEY RARE BREED

MGPUH-LEAZE

Many a fledgling American whiskey geek has become aghast upon learning that his favorite "craft" whiskey isn't produced at that quaint ol' warehouse down the road, but is instead sourced from a factory in Lawrenceburg, Indiana. As I've previously mentioned, Midwest Grain Products (or MGP), produces a good bulk of the supposedly small-brand whiskey in the country. And though it has twelve different whiskey mash bills including bourbon, wheat whiskey, and corn whiskey, its most famous recipe is for a 95% rye whiskey. I must admit, I love that rye. So, I figured, if a standard bottle of 95% MGP rye is pretty damn good, what if I combined several of them? The Smooth Ambler (at least 10 years old) adds maturity, James E. Pepper gives body and heat, and the Redemption youthful vibrancy. The odd pickle note of the Dickel means it should be used sparingly or else it throws off the whole blend.

Give this blend a cool name, slick label, and folksy marketing campaign and tell everybody you distilled it yourself until a class-action lawsuit forces you to come clean.

35% SMOOTH AMBLER OLD SCOUT LIMITED EDITION SINGLE BARREL RYE

20% REDEMPTION RYE

15% BULLEIT RYE

12% JAMES E. PEPPER "1776" STRAIGHT RYE BARREL PROOF

10% GEORGE DICKEL RYE WHISKY

8% ANGEL'S ENVY FINISHED RYE

THE FOUR POSEURS

There are three things you need to know about Four Roses Bourbon, and here's the tl;dr version. First, it is one of the most transparent companies in the whiskey world, completely forthright about what its mash bills consist of and how its blends are put together (and anything it doesn't outright reveal on its labels it'll gladly answer if you message the company through the website's contact form, which you presume no one ever reads). Second, unlike most other distilleries, which have a couple mash bills and one yeast strain, Four Roses has two bourbon mash bills and five yeast strains. That means (does the math on fingers) each barrel of Four Roses could be one of 10 recipes, all of which take the four-letter naming structure of O_S_. (An OBSQ Barrel, for example, would be a high-rye bourbon ["B"] with floral yeast notes ["Q"]. The "O" and "S" are immutable and stand for "Four Roses Distillery" and "straight whiskey.") The final thing you need to know about Four Roses is that, while its standard single-barrel release is the OBSV recipe, the other nine recipes can be obtained with a little hustle and effort courtesy of private barrel picks offered by some better stores like Binny's and Julio's. Put together a toolbox of all 10 recipes, and you, my friend, will now have immense power in your hands.

BARREL-STRENGTH YELLOW LABEL

Travis Hill wasn't the first to realize he could start making blends from his Four Roses barrel picks, but he was certainly the most thorough. Back in 2014, he had a hankering for a bottle of the much ballyhooed 2012 Limited Edition Small Batch. Released at a mere 4,000 bottles, unfortunately, by then it was selling for around $900 on the secondary market. For the sake of his bank account and credit line, he decided to try to blend the recipe himself using single-barrel bottles. The cost was a mere $300, and even Master Distiller Brent Elliott had to agree upon finally trying it that it was pretty good. In the following years, Hill has made more "poor man's" Four Roses LEs, as have countless other at-home enthusiasts. However, the Four Roses blend that I think is Hill's most interesting is this one.

Yellow Label is famously Four Roses' most low-level product, a $20 bottle in most states. And while whiskey geeks absolutely adore every single bottle that Four Roses releases, the same geeks pretty much ignore Yellow Label. Too harsh, too sharp a finish, too low proof. Hill decided to fix those problems by making Yellow Label at barrel strength. Yellow Label typically uses eight to nine of the ten recipes in its blend, and sometimes all ten, always at varying proportions depending on current stock and flavor profile. Here Hill simply uses 10% of each, which means 2.5 ounces of each will produce a full bottle.

10% FOUR ROSES SINGLE BARREL OBSF

10% FOUR ROSES SINGLE BARREL OBSK

10% FOUR ROSES SINGLE BARREL OBSO

10% FOUR ROSES SINGLE BARREL OBSQ

10% FOUR ROSES SINGLE BARREL OBSV

10% FOUR ROSES SINGLE BARREL OESF

10% FOUR ROSES SINGLE BARREL OESK

10% FOUR ROSES SINGLE BARREL OESO

10% FOUR ROSES SINGLE BARREL OESQ

10% FOUR ROSES SINGLE BARREL OESV

THE VITAMIX HACK

Meanwhile, Blake Riber of Poor Man's Pappy fame had been trying his own hand at making Four Roses Limited Editions. The only problem was, though he had the correct barrel recipes and ratios dialed in, they didn't taste that "close" to the originals. Then he talked to a Four Roses rep, who informed him their mixer "spews" the barrel when blending them, meaning the liquid is violently shot around. So Riber started throwing his Four Roses blends into a Vitamix on the  highest speed for a solid minute; it greatly improved his results. Dubbed "hyperdecanting" by chef and technologist Nathan Myhrvold, who uses the procedure on wine, the Vitamix blending is said to aggressively aerate the alcohol. The same hack works for bourbon, smoothing the rough edges of any poor man's blend.

RE-CREATED
PORT ELLEN

Steven Zeller is one of the founders of the Beast Masters Club, arranging single-barrel picks and fun tasting events for the mostly New York–based members. While the Beast Masters mainly focus on American whiskey, Zeller privately has a passion for Islay scotch, specifically those from Port Ellen. Unfortunately, if you know your whiskey history you'll know that Port Ellen closed its doors in 1983. Still, as recently as the early 2010s, Zeller was able to find bottles of its one-of-a-kind highly peated/ highly sherried offerings on store shelves and at reasonable prices. Today that's virtually impossible. So, like the many fans out there of so-called "ghost" distilleries, Zeller decided to see if he could re-create his beloved Port Ellen using products currently available. He wanted something big and smoky yet so smooth it would go down like silk. He thinks he finally found it.

60% LAGAVULIN 12 YEAR OLD

40% GLENDRONACH REVIVAL 15 YEAR OLD

PEAT 'N' GREET

Single-malt blends seem like a trickier nut to crack, but they're Kirk Sigurdson's specialty. A sci-fi novelist and creative writing professor in Portland, Oregon, he also blogs about brown juice under the name Whisky Kirk. Kirk likes to take quality older malts that have gone flat and blend them with younger, more virile malts. "This varies by whatever happens to be in my cabinet at the time," he told me. "I find that peaters are easiest to strike a balance with." He thinks making blends in miniature batches is easy; the real skill is duplicating them on a grander scale like, say, a Compass Box does commercially. Kirk calls the following his tried-and-true recipe, one that, by his calculus, creates a quality 750-milliliter bottle for a mere $30. Can't beat that.

67% BLACK & WHITE SCOTCH WHISKY

33% ARDBEG TEN YEAR OLD

SPLASH OF LAPHROAIG 10 YEAR OLD CASK STRENGTH

SMOKE SHOWS

One of the more ubiquitous styles of blending you'll find on the Internet today are "campfire" blends. The idea is based on David Perkins's avant-garde product introduced by High West in 2012. A fan not just of the American whiskey he would one day produce, Perkins had also fallen in love with smoky, peated Islay scotch while staying at the Bruichladdich distillery's bed and breakfast. There he found peat smoke was used for everything—cooking dinner, making desserts, stoking the fireplace. And it was always pleasant. So is his Campfire bottling, a blend of honey-sweet bourbon, florally-spiced rye, and smoky scotch. While High West Campfire is not all that hard to find on store shelves, whiskey geeks have chosen to follow Perkins's inspired idea by making campfire blends of their own. A few favorites I've both seen online and produced myself.

COCK IN A BOX

50% Compass Box The Peat Monster

50% Fighting Cock

FOUR OOGIES

33.3% Four Roses Single Barrel

33.3% O.K.I. Rye Reserve

33.3% Ardbeg Uigeadail

KENTUCKY BY THE SEA

50% Rittenhouse Rye

35% W.L. Weller Special Reserve

15% Talisker Storm

DOC OCTO-DAD

50% Old Grand-Dad 114

35% Octomore

15% Old Crow*

S'MORES 'ROUND THE FIRE

50% Redbreast 12 Year Old (your marshmallow)

20% Prichard's Double Chocolate Bourbon

15% Angel's Envy Finished Rye (your graham cracker)

15% Ardbeg Corryvreckan (your fire)

*James C. Crow was a doctor; hence the blend's clever name. He also may have invented the sour mash process, but you don't care.

BOTANICAL BLENDS

Gin and whiskey are often at odds with each other. In fact, it's virtually impossible to name a prominent cocktail where both spirits are listed in the starting lineup. Perhaps the most famous, if you could call it that, is the Suffering Bastard, a late-1940s libation with bourbon, gin, Angostura bitters, lime juice, and ginger ale that was known as a hangover cure. Despite their ignominious history together, I wanted to see if I could add just a kiss of gin to a whiskey to make for a botanical-filled product that actually worked. Ultimately I learned the best gin to use is one already fairly similar to whiskey—in other words, barrel-aged—while the best whiskeys are ones that already have a decent amount of minty and dill-like herbal notes that play well with botanicals.

55% SAZERAC RYE

35% GEORGE DICKEL RYE WHISKY

10% BLUECOAT BARREL FINISHED GIN

Another botanicalish blend that works well involves placing peaty Islay scotch with aged aquavit, a combo Leo Robitschek of Manhattan's NoMad Bar has successfully integrated into his cocktails. In this case the Danish aquavit adds some pleasant dill, fennel, caraway, and even anise notes as well as a slight oloroso sherry kiss.

85% LAGAVULIN 16 YEAR OLD

15% LYSHOLM LINIE AQUAVIT

BOTANICAL BLEND AND TONIC (BB&T)

MAKES 1 COCKTAIL

There's no point in making a ridiculous botanical whiskey if you're not going to turn it into an easy-drinking highball on occasion.

2 OUNCES BOTANICAL BLEND (RECIPES PRECEDE)

FEVER-TREE ELDERFLOWER TONIC WATER

FLAMED ORANGE PEEL, FOR GARNISH

Pour the Botanical Blend into a Collins glass filled with ice cubes. Top with tonic to taste. Flame an orange peel and garnish the cocktail. Sit on a porch and drink all day.

ADDITIONAL BLENDS TO EXPLORE

MAY/DECEMBER

You're using: Something super old and something super young (probably that craft whiskey you bought for $90 whose age statement is measured in months, not years). Can you use the older product to bring maturity to the younger? Maybe the younger can add some vibrancy to the old dog, who is getting a little lifeless.

WOODY WOODPECKER

You're using: The woodiest whiskeys on your shelf, like that Old Blowhard 26 Year Old you paid a ton for. Add it to the other oak bombs in your collection to feel what it must be like to drink straight sawdust.

LUCK OF THE IRISH

You're using: All the cheap Irish whiskey you have, seeing if there is power (or Powers) in numbers.

PENNSYLTUCKY

You're using: Kentucky bourbon and Pennsylvania rye.

MAKING AN AGE STATEMENT

You're using: Exclusively whiskeys age stated from one particular year. So all 10-year-olds or all 12-year-olds, or all 30-year-olds if you're crazy. Do you suspect one year is the best year for a whiskey to be aged? Well, then, go with that!

HAZARDOUS MATERIALS

You're using: All hazmat-level whiskeys— in other words, products over 140 proof, which makes them potentially flammable and not allowed to travel with you on commercial flights.

GRAPES AND GRAIN

You're using: Mostly whiskey but also a little cognac or Armagnac. Also try an Apple Grain blend with calvados and/or apple brandy. Blake Riber actually thinks simply doing a cognac or Armagnac "rinse" of the glass before adding your whiskey is best.

WADE WOODARD'S

THE BARREL REFILL PROJECT

While some dudes are pussyfooting around with mixing an ounce here and an ounce there, others are going full throttle. Forget making your own bottle of home-blended booze; how 'bout an entire damn barrel, sometimes called "super-vatting"? Wade Woodard decided to make his own brash salvo after scoring an empty Eagle Rare barrel (I told you empty barrels would eventually play a part in this book). His vision was to fill the 53-gallon barrel about halfway, as he would get better oxidation (and thus barrel aging) that way. He enlisted 10 other enthusiasts, so, despite the overall project cost of $1,650, each person had to pony up only $150. Not bad for a three-year experiment. Woodard tested the initial recipe at the single-serving level first, and you can as well, assuming you don't have a spare barrel and 10 friends.

39% (18 HANDLES) TOM MOORE BOTTLED IN BOND

39% (18 HANDLES) VERY OLD BARTON 86 PROOF

11% (TWELVE 750-MILLILITER BOTTLES) OLD GRAND-DAD 114

11% (TWELVE 750-MILLILITER BOTTLES) STAGG JR.

Fill the barrel and place it in a fairly cool, dark place (Woodard stored his barrel in a friend's air-conditioned garage in Houston). Test every year for up to three years. While the batch started at just around 100 proof, by the time Woodard pulled it, it was 106. About one-third had been lost to the angel's share, and the profile was now very floral.

THE OLD BALDY BLEND

Even more badass than The Barrel Refill Project is the story of Old Baldy, Ed Bley and Jeff Mattingly's multibarrel blend. Ed Bley is the acclaimed spirits and beer manager for Cork 'n Bottle, a top bottle shop in northern Kentucky. He's famous for picking and selling dozens of single-barrel offerings per year, many with sourcing help from Mattingly, the owner of Bourbon 30 Spirits. In 2017 they decided to examine 35 of these single-barrel purchases and blend them into a one-of-a-kind offering. The result was Old Baldy, a blend of mostly 11-year-old and 8-year-old stock from three unnamed distilleries in Kentucky and Indiana. This house blend produced a mere 320 bottles, which were sold for $109.99 exclusively at Cork n' Bottle. The few people who tasted it claim it's everything from a "freak show of flavor" (Bourbon & Banter) to "all my favorite characteristics in bourbon" (Superfly Bourbon Club). If you got a spare 35 barrels lying around yourself, I encourage you to try the craziest, and priciest, amateur blend of them all.

CHAPTER 3

INFINITY BOTTLES

BLENDING
WITHOUT PREJUDICE

The infinity bottle is the ultimate amateur blend. As in the world of sherry, where casks are fractionally blended over time via the solera system to create a continuous consistency, and infinity bottle is a designated bottle you will continually add spirits to and blend together to create a living *inconsistency*. Also known as a "solera bottle" or "fractional bottle" or even a "living bottle," it seems to have first entered prominence courtesy of a 2012 video by popular whiskey vlogger Ralfy Mitchell (please don't say "vlogger"). In his thick brogue, this undertaker from the Isle of Man explains that the infinity bottle is the only whiskey an amateur can create that is 100% uniquely his or her own. Not only that, but he thinks it's part of one's whiskey, if not overall spirit-drinking, history. Loftier than even that, Ralfy claims an infinity bottle could eventually become a family heirloom, like Grandpa's war medals or that one picture of Mom at Graceland.

The rules of infinity bottles are truly yours and yours alone. Some people think you should use only the same category of spirit. You start with a bourbon and continue with bourbons and bourbons only. You start with a blended Irish whiskey, don't add Scottish single malts too. Others, me included, think a certain helter-skelterness is what truly makes infinity bottles interesting.

In my own infinity bottle—which is a decanter my wife and I received as a wedding gift and never knew what to do with—I toss in the last ounce or so of pretty much every whiskey I drink. Bourbon, rye, Taiwanese and Japanese whiskies, heavily peated scotch, sherry-finished products, well-aged stuff, and even young craft whiskeys that kind of suck. Some people aren't afraid to even throw in other spirits—gin, mezcal, some obscure amaro, you name it. I've learned that even a half ounce of peated whiskey can overtake an entire infinity bottle, and a gin's botanicals almost always mess up the entire vat, but since an infinity bottle is always changing, you'll eventually drink those negatives out. And that's part of the fun.

It sounds ridiculous, but it can be truly surprising how good a final (or "current") product you can inadvertently create. Super complex, obviously, but often super tasty too. Of course, the flavor changes heavily over the years. As one infinity bottle advocate told me, "Sometimes it's unfocused and fuzzy; sometimes it's goddamn on point." No surprise, many infinity bottlers like him have grown quite emotionally attached to their bottles. Why wouldn't they? They're truly one-of-a-kind and literally impossible to ever re-create. You can always buy another bottle of that Pappy you just finished, but if you have a brilliant sip from your infinity bottle—that's it.

At the least, it's a very, very easy way to play with your whiskey. Because there's really no such thing as an infinity failure. And that's the best part.

THE H∞FINITY BOTTLE

In the whiskey world, like the real world, every action needs an equal and opposite reaction. If people love a certain product (or idea) way too much, you'll immediately start seeing a groundswell of people who hate it just as passionately. Thus, with infinity bottles picking

up steam as of late, a snarky rejoinder needed to appear. Enter the Hatefinity Bottle or H∞finity Bottle or H8finity Bottle. Whatever you call it, it's just what it sounds like, an infinity bottle composed strictly of whiskeys you truly loathed. Instead of pouring those bad boys down the drain, or saving them for less-cherished visitors as you might have in the past, add them to your decanter. With any luck, the combined hate will create a lovely blend.

HOW TO GO TO INFINITY AND BEYOND

While Ralfy Mitchell is methodical about how he builds his infinity bottle, tweaking and testing everything before eventually adding a new pour, many others choose to live dangerously, tossing the final ounces of any and every bottle they own into their mix just to see what happens. As German infinity bottler Helmut Barro told me, "I began to appreciate the work of professional blenders and how difficult it is to keep up a continuous taste experience for a customer. With each new addition to my infinity bottle, the taste actually changes—sometimes for the good, sometimes for the weird. Sometimes it's very pronounced, sometimes barely noticeable."

You hardly need instructions to create such an improvised blend, yet here they are.

● ●

1. Procure an empty bottle—a classy decanter you got for your wedding but have never known what to do with (just make sure it has a cap that seals well), a particularly fetching empty bottle you've never had the heart to throw out, or even a brand-new bottle that can be ordered from a number of online retailers (but probably ordered from Amazon because that's where everyone orders everything).

2. Affix a clean white label to the back (unless your wife is really attached to that crystal decanter; in that case maybe just use a nearby piece of paper). You will use this to keep a running tally of each new whiskey you add along with the date.

3. Have a loose strategy for what you are going to add to the infinity bottle. The first ounce of every new whiskey bottle you open? The final ounce of every bottle you've almost finished (a great way to allow a great bottle to live on forever)? Only the  best of the bests you taste, as a nice way to honor cherished "fallen soldiers"? The choice is up to you.

4. Once your infinity bottle has finally become full, allow it to sit for a few days, give it a swirl, and have a try. If it sucks, well, no big deal; that's literally the only time it will taste that way.

5. Replace the ounces you just drank with new ounces from another bottle. As Ralfy says, "Every time I pour a wee dram out of it, I put another wee dram into it."

6. Pass along this bottle to your offspring upon your untimely death, who will think you are weird for having a "living" bottle.

• •

A BRIEF NOTE ON THE SAFETY OF DECANTERS, AS RECOMMENDED BY MY HIGH-POWERED LEGAL TEAM

It's all fun and games, until you get lead poisoning. Unfortunately, many of the handsome crystal decanters on the market are actually lead-based.

Why would wholesome, well-meaning companies put something so dangerous on the market? Because they don't expect you to fill their decanters with high-proof whiskey. Despite what television has led us to believe, most people fill decanters with wine, not whiskey. Many wines need time to breathe, and putting them in a decanter does just that. Wine  likewise isn't high proof enough to allow lead to leach from the walls of the decanter, especially in the hour or so it takes you to decant and finish the wine. You're not going to finish a decanter of whiskey in an hour, however, and if your infinity bottle is sitting in a decanter for months, its high-octane liquid is most definitely pulling lead from it. In just a day or two, a potentially dangerous amount could end up in your infinity liquid. It will be a family heirloom passed down to the next generation quicker than you ever imagined.

So, how to know if your decanter is made of lead. Well . . .

- Check the box it came in, dummy. Sadly, even that beauty from Waterford crystal is likely to be made of like 25% lead.

- Hold it up to the light. A leaded decanter will typically cause a "rainbow effect" when light is refracted through it. This isn't always the case, but if you see the rainbow, lead poisoning is a possibility.

- If your decanter is labeled as "plain pressed glass," it is probably fine. It's also probably a cheap decanter and ugly but, whatever, you're still living another day.

NOTE: Some folks claim you can "preleach" lead out of a leaded decanter by first filling it with a 50/50 mixture of vinegar and vodka for 24 hours, but, uh, caveat emptor.

A FEW RECOMMENDED INFINITIES

Personally, I think it's good not to have a strict system for making your infinity bottle, but it can be fun to follow a certain aesthetic. In other words, fill your infinity bottle with unmeasured, random amounts each time—but try to focus on a certain infinity genre at the least. Here are a few suggestions to get you started.

THE BRAND X INFINITY

Maybe you're obsessed with Jim Beam. Or you're a nut for Macallan (I'm sorry, *THE* Macallan). Perhaps you love Jack Daniel's so much you have

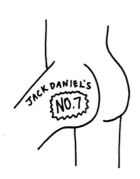

the logo tattooed on your left ass cheek. If there's a particular whiskey brand you love more than any other, try making an infinity bottle with its products and only its products. Old vintages, each new releases, special single-barrel picks, and even the pricey limited editions. This can allow you to see the similarities among a distillery's entire line while also creating its most complex blend ever made. The symbiosis among a brand's offerings means these almost always work well.

THE PARADE OF ROSES

One of the more famous underground single-brand infinity bottles is

Travis Hill's all–Four Roses one, which he claims has at least 60 different bottles in it all told.

THE SINGLE-MALT SOLERA

You're one of those guys who has the complete opposite of a slobby man cave. You have a "study." And in it are boxes and tubes and fancy wood cases of expensive single malt. If you're one of those classy gents, you probably also have your own decanter. Start dumpin' a dram of every single malt into it. Should you focus on a region? A Speyside-only solera? A Highlands-mostly infinity? I'm not sure that's necessary, though you'll have to be careful when it comes to including peated whiskies, which can absolutely torch a well-built blend . . .

THE ISLAY INFINITY

. . . which is why this is a solera niche worth separating. Islay is, in my opinion, the site of the world's finest whiskey. But, yes, it's also the peatiest, the smokiest, the most likely to make your vodka-swilling friends gag and to make others start thinking you've just lit some medical gauze on fire. There are only eight distilleries currently on the island, and debates continually abound over which is best. Whether you think it's Laphroaig or Lagavulin, Ardbeg or Bruichladdich, Bowmore or Caol Ila . . . you're not wrong. They're all the best. And that's why this potent infinity blend will rule.

THE BONDED INFINITY

One thing I've found that doesn't work great in infinity blends is using whiskeys that are too low proof. Forget that 80-proof noise. They simply get dulled out by the rest of the musicians in the solera band. That's why a fun challenge is using only bonded whiskeys. Whether bourbon or rye, these 100-proof products are usually cheap, readily available, and perfect at playing with each other. You can even throw in a little bonded applejack if you'd like to sweeten things up.

THE CASK-STRENGTH INFINITY

Or why not just go all the way and use only the highest-proof products in your collection, ones that have never been cut by water? Cask-strength scotch, barrel-proof bourbon, this infinity bottle might melt the glass it's held in.

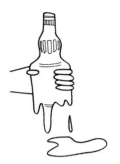

THE GINFINITY BOTTLE

Maybe whiskey isn't your thing (Why are you reading this book? Please return it to its rightful owner). My friend Chloe Frechette likes whiskey—and has a whiskey infinity bottle—but she also digs gin. Therefore she also keeps a self-dubbed ginfinity bottle. I think that's a clever name, and I'm a dad, so I wanted to include it here.

THE LIVING BARREL

This is only for people who are truly crazy. Instead of an infinity bottle, this is your infinity *barrel*. Instead of merely adding a splash or so of every whiskey bottle in your collection, you will be glugging mostly full bottles down the bunghole. Of course, you will also be imparting added aging and barrel character to your blend. You will lose some alcohol to evaporation, and the proof might even rise. And your neighbors will quietly talk about you behind your back. Better that than them calling the ATF.

CHAPTER 4

FINISHING

IT'S NOT DONE
'TIL YOU SAY IT IS

I've already discussed the vast world of terrible gifts you can get a whiskey lover, like a moonshine-"aging" kit. Any true connoisseur clearly recognizes that using a teeny tiny barrel to age lackluster white dog is not going to result in anything all too palatable—certainly not something better than anything already in his or her collection. But what if you could take one of these (admittedly super cute) tiny barrels and merely use it to *finish* an already solid whiskey? Yes, many whiskey lovers have begun to do just that.

The idea of finishing whiskey is said to have begun in 1983, when Balvenie put some already oak-aged scotch into sherry butts for a few additional months. However, the person many credit with taking finishing to the next level is Dr. Bill Lumsden. Through his work as master distiller at both Glenmorangie and Ardbeg, he has experimented with finishing whiskey in everything from Côte de Nuits wine barrels to Pedro Ximenez sherry barrels to even extra-porous American oak casks. He claims it's not just the wood, but rather the "in-drink"—the smidge of previous liquid absorbed in the barrel—that is most crucial to the whiskey's future flavor profile.

Today, finishing whiskey is no longer seen as an only rarely used gimmick. In fact, whiskeys on both sides of the pond are being finished (or undergoing, ahem, "secondary maturation") in everything from sherry butts to port casks to Sauternes hogsheads to rum barrels to even gold bars in the case of Gold Bar Gold Whiskey, which I swear is not a joke. If, in the last few years, barrel-aged cocktails have become a popular bar item thanks to noted bartender Jeffrey Morgenthaler, the world of DIY finishes is still strictly the domain of the at-home tinkerer. And that's a good thing.

While it may or may not be legal for a bar to add its own barrel finishes, it certainly wouldn't be financially savvy. But home collectors, perhaps bored with their collections, perhaps trying to create buzz among their friends, are experimenting with unique finishes they think (they hope!) might improve an already-bottled whiskey. While there's obviously plenty of allure in "super-sizing," if you will, an already great whiskey, a port-finished Pappy is probably better in theory than actuality (although it would surely be boffo for your Instagram likes and follower comments).

Still, my thinking has always been that there are already plenty of great wine-finished whiskeys on the market. Why not do finishes the professionals would never even dare?

DR. BILL LUMSDEN

—

With a PhD in microbial physiology and fermentation science, Dr. Bill Lumsden is one of the preeminent minds in the scotch world, developing products for two major brands. As the director of distilling, whisky creation, and whisky stocks for the Glenmorangie company (man, his business card must be in really small print), he creates products for both Glenmorangie and Ardbeg. Many of his career highlights have been in the world of finishing and secondary maturation, with such visionary creations as his Glenmorangie Malaga and Margaux Wood Finish(es) and Ardbeg Uigeadail (highly smoky whisky finished in ex-sherry casks). In his own words on the subject . . .

We've had huge success over the years with our wood management program. That certainly has been my main claim to fame with Glenmorangie. All the different cask types, all the different oak types we have used.

Did we invent it? I don't know . . .

I inherited the fledgling wood program, including fledgling attempts at finishing, from my predecessor, Neil McKerrow. What I did was kind of resurrect the whole thing because it wasn't going anywhere and the company hadn't been willing to invest in it.

(Again, I know our friends at a certain company in Speyside have a massive chip on their shoulder about being the first to do everything you can think of. I think they put the first man on the moon as well!)

The reality is, over the years, over the decades, many people would have taken whisky from one barrel and thought, "this is not very good." Then they might have put it into another barrel in an attempt to give it a second life. So, we'll never really know who actually invented finishing. But one thing is for certain, the Glenmorangie company was the first to commercialize the idea, the first to actually talk about it.

What we've certainly discovered over the years, is that it's not just a case of buying yet another wine cask and putting your whisky in that and then automatically getting a good product. I've tasted some utterly appalling examples of the genre. Brendan (McCarron, my right-hand man) and I would have never allowed many of these to be bottled because they just don't work.

One of the main things I've learned is certain types of oak can be very unforgiving. There was a shortage of wood in Scotland three or four years ago, the number of bourbon barrels coming over here was much lower, the prices were much higher, and I know for a fact that many distillers were just buying old French oak wine casks and putting their new spirit into it. In 12 years' time they'll be in for a big shock! It is a very unforgiving wood.

I bought some Hungarian Tokay casks ages ago. Ages before any other distiller in Scotland had them. After six months it was absolutely sublime, fragrant, and aromatic. And for whatever reason I took my eye off the ball, left the whisky in for too long, and after two and a half years it was completely ruined. That was a hard lesson to learn. To this day, it annoys me.

Sampling is the real key to finishing. That's not always easy in a big distillery, though. Especially since a lot of our stock now isn't palletized. If you're building a new warehouse, unless it's a warehouse specifically built for (sherry) butts, which you need to put on racks, or dunnage, you palletize it, because you can fit double the stock in there. But if they're on pallets, it's not easy to get to them for tastings.

Mentally, there's no real exercise I go through when it comes to finishing. I'm not a massively cerebral distiller. I'm a visceral person, and it's more a gut feeling for me. And this is what I've always said to Brendan: I can't teach him anything about distilling, and I can't teach you either. With years of experience, and getting to know your brands, 99 times out of 100, with my first sniff I just know whether something's good or bad. It's an instant reaction.

Finishes don't always work with heavily peated whisky for instance. You're looking for a fairly subtle, complementary change. By its very nature, you're looking to not lose the house character of the whisky. But if you've got heavily peated whisky, sometimes a finish for 12 to 18 months will make very little difference. Or, what can sometimes also happen—I've tasted this in one or two whiskies over the years—the combination of a very rich and sticky sherry cask and a heavily peated whisky can be quite cloying.

On the other hand, with nonpeated whisky, you're not necessarily looking to bolster the flavor; you're looking to perhaps set it off down a different path. The trick for us is to make sure we maintain enough of the house character of the whisky. So for Glenmorangie we have to be careful, like the Tokay example. You leave it in too long, you just lose it.

The best thing about secondary maturation is you can buy barrels and have a new product on the shelf in two years. If you're changing things like barley variety, the way you mash, or yeasts during primary production, it's going to take a decade or more to learn if that worked. But finishing is a quick experiment. That's why I like it so much.

HOW TO FINISH

As with most of our experiments in this book, higher-proof spirits are better and quicker at extracting barrel character. So opt for bottled-in-bond bourbons or cask-strength offerings for finishing (some of which have been recommended on pages 86–90).

●●●

1. Procure a 1- or 2-liter barrel from an online vendor, although if you have the funds to go bigger (say, 5 or even 10 liters), you will get better-quality, less-woody finishes. (Having said that, the bigger the barrel, the more finishing liquid you will have to initially add and the more time your whiskey will need to spend in the barrel.)

2. "Cure" your barrel by filling it with water, then emptying it several times to clear out any wood debris. Then fill it with hot water and leave it to sit on top of a towel for a couple of days. This will swell the wood until there are no leaks.

3. Condition or "season" the wood for a couple days or a few weeks by fully filling the barrel, whatever its size, with another spirit, wine, cocktail, or liquid. If you're a cheapskate, choose something you won't mind drinking once it is removed from the barrel!

4. After dumping (and hopefully drinking) the liquid in the barrel, add your whiskey of choice. Roll the barrel a bit, then leave it to sit for at least five days. Barrels have historically always been stored on their sides, although of late distilleries have begun keeping them upright for space concerns.

5. Carefully monitor the progress of the whiskey from day to day by tasting to discern any new flavor developments.

6. If using a 1- or 2-liter barrel, you should have finished whiskey after 5 to 10 days. It should be darker than it was initially. Perhaps a tad oxidized. Of course, if you're a quick-drinking lush, you can keep it in the barrel and drink drams straight from the spigot, although it is probably better to empty it into a bottle or a lead-free decanter.

7. Taste your new creation—hopefully you'll actually want to finish what you just finished.

8. Clean the barrel if you wish, with a vodka rinse or a special cleaning solution, by soaking it for 24 hours, emptying it, and then rinsing three times with scalding-hot water. (You can likewise attempt to rechar your barrel by placing a butane torch through the bunghole. Be careful!) Now try again.

• •

On the following pages are a few recommended finishes to help you get started. For each, assume a 1-liter barrel, with 1 liter's worth of finishing liquid, and adjust from there. As Dr. Bill Lumsden has mentioned, finishing can be a very "touchy-feely" thing since both the whiskey and barrels are so unpredictable. Thus, there are no hard and fast rules when it comes to timing; it's simply up to you to find what works!

COMMON FINISHES

The following are a few of the more common whiskey finishes, all of which have been done regularly by many commercial whiskey distilleries over the years. Flat out: *They work.* The better the product you use to season your barrel, the better the quality of the finish you'll get. But not *that* much better, and therefore many folks are willing to sacrifice a little flavor so they don't have to use a $2,000 VSOP cognac to season their barrel.

SHERRY

Great cheap option: Lustau

The most common finish in the scotch industry, it also works well with American whiskey, especially rye. Anywhere from five to eight days will turn the whiskey darker and fruitier, balancing out any spicier notes.

RUBY PORT

Great cheap option: Sandeman

Try to make a "poor man's" version of High West's A Midwinter Night's Dram—a port- and French oak–finished rye—by aging a higher-proof rye like Rittenhouse for a week.

COGNAC

Great cheap option: Hennessy VS

A cognac finish adds a nice light fruitiness to more delicate whiskeys. It also sounds classy as shit.

WINE

Great cheap option: Whatever you drank a glass of and then didn't finish the bottle

Red wine preferred, but whites can add some cool characteristics too. Sauternes and Madeira wine have become increasingly popular experimental finishes of late as well.

SWEET VERMOUTH

Great cheap option: Dolin Vermouth de Chambéry Rouge

Everyone has bought a giant bottle of sweet vermouth before, made a couple Manhattans, and then watched helplessly as the bottle slowly began oxidizing, the cap soldering onto the neck in a sickly syrupy mess. Before it gets too out of hand, dump it in the barrel. The dark fruits, winey, and slightly oxidized notes will work well with a scotch or a Japanese whisky, adding a refined, mature edge to the product.

AGED RUM

Great cheap option: Appleton Estate Rare Blend 12 Year Old

While an aged rum is typically used for finishing—and is likewise what would have actually come out of a barrel—playing around with an incredibly funky, high-ester Jamaican white rum (like Wray & Nephew Overproof or Rum Fire) can also lead to some fun results and amp up the complexities to 11.

OFFBEAT OPTIONS

A few of the following have been attempted by more offbeat distilleries, usually of the American craft variety. Many of these, however, do not have a commercially made, widely released analogue as far as I have seen. Nevertheless, they can work!

APPLE BRANDY

Great cheap option: Laird's Apple Brandy 100
Adds a nice apple pie–like note to more vanillin-heavy bourbons.

IMPERIAL STOUTS/BARLEY WINES

Great cheap option: Goose Island Bourbon County Brand Stout/J.W. Lees Harvest Ale
Of late, beer-barrel finishing has become somewhat popular, with distilleries as big as Jameson and Glenfiddich getting into the game. Personally I don't think it does much, but it can be fun to play around with. Opt for a barrel-aged stout, which means you'll be finishing your whiskey in a beer that has already been finished in a whiskey barrel itself. Kinda like an ouroboros of barrel aging, if you will. Barrel-aged barley wines work nicely as well, especially those of the rich and refined English variety like J.W. Lees. Those can add even stronger caramel, leather, and oxidized notes, which will likewise "mature" the whiskey somewhat.

ICE WINE

Great cheap option: Very few

I've always liked drinking that sort of
sickly sweet dessert wine that will have
the more respectable winos at the dinner
table mocking you. Alas, even if you don't

like drinking it, it can add a nice finishing note to milder scotches and
Irish whiskeys, even upping the richness somewhat. Try a Tokay as well,
the Hungarian/Slovak sweet wine that Dr. Bill Lumsden once tried (and
failed) with.

AMARO

Great cheap option: Amaro Montenegro

Now we're cooking with gas. Adding an amaro to the barrel will create a
finish that will almost turn your whiskey into a bottled cocktail. "Monte,"
with its slightly sweet orange peel and dark cherry notes, works
particularly well with a variety of whiskeys.

FERNET

Great cheap option: Fernet-Branca

Even more muscular than Monte, Fernet is a love-it-or-leave-it amaro
for many folks. Able to outmuscle just about anything it comes into
contact with, Fernet is best used simply as a quick "rinse"—fill and then
shake the barrel. Then, opt for a prodigious dram to battle it out—cask-
strength rye whiskey or a heavily peated scotch is your best bet. Another
option is Branca Menta, Fernet's minty cousin, which can add a fantastic
Christmas twist to sweeter bourbons.

AÑEJO TEQUILA

Great cheap option: Espolòn

While having a tequila-finished whiskey sounds cool, tequila finishing honestly doesn't do much. Opt for a light, more delicate and floral Irish whiskey or scotch for this experiment. You want to use something that will not overpower the beautiful agave notes.

MEZCAL

Great cheap option: Del Maguey Vida de San Luis del Rio

Mezcal makes for perhaps the most fun finish there is, though it ain't cheap. Go smoke on smoke by finishing a particularly peaty pour in a particularly smoky mezcal. Or bolster a sweet southwest-style whiskey (Balcones or maybe Whiskey Del Bac) with a hint of mezcal from our beloved neighbors to the south. As a bonus, you can add some barrel notes to an unaged mezcal to calm it down a bit.

MUSCAT-FINISHED RYE

It's not just at-home geeks who are doing crazy things with whiskey. Quite a few avant-garde craft distilleries are advancing the cause as well. Like High West, which differentiated itself early on with both interesting blends and intriguing finishes, many of which were available only in small quantities at their Park City gift shop. High West has done vermouth finishes, Campfire finishes, and even cocktail barrel finishes (something we'll look at ourselves on page 98), but David Perkins tells me he has most loved their random dessert wine finishes. "You're not going to find bottles today, but someone is enjoying them somewhere," he jokes.

Well, if we can't commercially buy them anymore, then at least we can try to re-create them. Perkins's two favorites have come from Muscat barrels, a sweet, floral, and multicolored series of grape varieties mostly from France and Italy. High West's Double Rye!, finished in orange Muscat barrels was quite flowery and, as Perkins explains, smelled like orange blossoms.

1 LITER QUADY ESSENSIA ORANGE MUSCAT

1 LITER HIGH WEST DOUBLE RYE!

Fill your 1-liter barrel with the Muscat and allow it to soak overnight, rotating occasionally. Empty the barrel the next day. Fill the barrel with Double Rye! or another rye of your choosing. Taste starting on day 5, monitoring until you are pleased with the flavor profile.

THE JULIUS

MAKES 1 COCKTAIL

This flip variant should have the texture, if not the flavor profile, of an Orange Julius you would have gotten at the mall in the 1970s.

1½ OUNCES ORANGE MUSCAT–FINISHED RYE (RECIPE PRECEDES)

½ OUNCE COINTREAU

½ OUNCE VANILLA SYRUP (MAKE THE SYRUP BY HEATING UP EQUAL AMOUNTS OF WATER AND SUGAR WITH A WHOLE VANILLA BEAN; LET IT COOL BEFORE STRAINING)

2 DASHES ANGOSTURA ORANGE BITTERS

1 WHOLE EGG

2 TEASPOONS HEAVY CREAM

ORANGE TWIST, FOR GARNISH

Pour all the ingredients into a shaker and shake until frothy, then add ice and shake again. Strain into a chilled rocks glass. Express the orange twist over the drink and use as a garnish.

COLD BREW-FINISHED SINGLE MALT

High West's brother in playing with firewater might be Virginia Distillery Company. Started by an Irish immigrant in central Virginia's Blue Ridge Mountains— "... Shenandoah River," uh, sorry—the company has released mostly Highlands-sourced scotch in its early years. It was able to make those bottlings uniquely its own through a variety of intriguing finishes.

With the Virginia-Highland Whisky series, they've experimented with finishing techniques using products from other local artisans like port-style wine, Chardonnay, and even cider. The first one that really made me sit up, however, was the Coffee Finished Virginia-Highland Whisky, a limited single-cask bottling made to honor and raise money for Nelson County first responders, who had recently battled a forest fire that raged on a hillside near the distillery. Virginia Distillery Company used a cold brew from local Trager Brothers Coffee to soak a barrel. Once finished in that barrel, the Highland Whisky picked up additional notes of cocoa, baking spices, and, of course, coffee.

8 OUNCES FRESHLY ROASTED LOCAL COFFEE BEANS

1 LITER VIRGINIA HIGHLAND SINGLE MALT WHISKY (ONE THAT HASN'T BEEN PREVIOUSLY FINISHED)

Grind the beans and make at least 1 liter of cold brew. (I like the Toddy Cold Brew System, but any is fine.) Fill your 1-liter barrel with cold brew and allow it to soak overnight, rotating the barrel occasionally. Empty the barrel the next day and enjoy a glass of oak-aged cold brew. Fill the barrel with whisky. Taste starting on day 5, monitoring until you are pleased with the flavor profile. Feel free to test with other styles of whiskey and other varieties of coffee beans.

WHISKY FOR BREAKFAST

MAKES 1 COCKTAIL

Who says bottomless mimosas and baroque Bloodys are the only acceptable breakfast cocktail? This Manhattan variant makes for the perfect "mornin's morning."

1½ OUNCES COLD BREW–FINISHED SINGLE MALT (RECIPE PRECEDES)

1 OUNCE SWEET VERMOUTH

1½ TEASPOONS BROWN SUGAR AND CINNAMON SYRUP (MAKE THE SYRUP BY HEATING UP EQUAL AMOUNTS OF WATER AND BROWN SUGAR, WITH 2 CINNAMON STICKS; LET IT COOL BEFORE STRAINING)

3 DASHES ANGOSTURA ORANGE BITTERS

1 BACON SLICE OR ORANGE WHEEL, FOR GARNISH

Pour the ingredients into a mixing glass with ice and stir until chilled. Strain into a chilled coupe and garnish with a bacon slice or orange wheel.

COCKTAIL FINISHING

You can add even more complexity to your finishes by first aging a cocktail in the barrel. The bonus here is that you can actually enjoy the cocktail while waiting for your whiskey to finish, uh *finishing*. I've tried aging all sorts of cocktails in barrels, everything from martinis to negronis to even an ill-advised Long Island Iced Tea. These are a few favorites that also work well with finishing whiskey. Again, the recipes are based on 1-liter barrels.

MANHATTAN-FINISHED RITTENHOUSE

Makes around 10 cocktails

22 OUNCES WILD TURKEY 101 BOURBON OR RYE

11 OUNCES DOLIN VERMOUTH DE CHAMBÉRY ROUGE

½ OUNCE ANGOSTURA BITTERS

1 LITER RITTENHOUSE RYE (OR ANOTHER BONDED OR OVERPROOF RYE)

Pour the Wild Turkey, vermouth, and the bitters into the barrel to build a Manhattan. Age the cocktail for at least one week, testing thereafter to find the flavor profile you like. Then empty the barrel and enjoy a cocktail in a chilled coupe with an orange twist garnish. Add the Rittenhouse Rye to the barrel and age for one to two weeks.

BOULEVARDIER-FINISHED RUSSELL'S

Makes around 10 cocktails

11 OUNCES OLD OVERHOLT

11 OUNCES CAMPARI

11 OUNCES CARPANO ANTICA FORMULA

1 LITER RUSSELL'S RESERVE SINGLE BARREL RYE

Pour the Old Overholt, Campari, and Carpano into the barrel to build a Boulevardier. Age the cocktail for at least one week, testing thereafter to find the flavor profile you like. Then empty the barrel and enjoy a cocktail in a rocks glass with a giant ice cube and an orange twist garnish. Add the Russell's Reserve Single Barrel Rye to the barrel and age from three days to one week. The strong Campari notes can quickly ruin a finish if you're not careful.

VIEUX CARRÉ-FINISHED STAGG JR.

While not as famed as the aforementioned cocktails, many bartenders believe the Vieux Carré is the most superior cocktail for barrel aging.

Makes around 8 cocktails

8 OUNCES HIGH WEST DOUBLE RYE!

8 OUNCES LOUIS ROYER PRÉFÉRENCE VSOP COGNAC

8 OUNCES COCCHI STORICO VERMOUTH DI TORINO

1½ OUNCES BÉNÉDICTINE

½ OUNCE ANGOSTURA BITTERS

½ OUNCE PEYCHAUD'S BITTERS

1 LITER STAGG JR.

Pour the rye, cognac, vermouth, bénédctine, and both bitters into the barrel to build a Vieux Carré. Age the cocktail for at least one week, testing thereafter to find the flavor profile you like. Then empty the barrel and enjoy a cocktail in a rocks glass with a giant ice cube and a lemon garnish. Add the Stagg Jr. to the barrel and age for one to two weeks.

LONG ISLAND–FINISHED ISLANDER

This is the barrel-aged cocktail that will make your friends ask, "You did what?!" Finishing a quality whiskey in there afterward might have them checking you for concussion symptoms.

Makes around 10 to 11 cocktails

6 OUNCES PLYMOUTH GIN

6 OUNCES REYKA VODKA

6 OUNCES RUM FIRE

6 OUNCES ESPOLÒN BLANCO

6 OUNCES COINTREAU

3 OUNCES CARAVELLA LIMONCELLO

1 LITER TALISKER STORM

SPLASH OF COLA

Pour the gin, vodka, rum, Espolòn, Cointreau, and limoncello into the barrel to build a Long Island Iced Tea. Age the cocktail for at least one week, testing thereafter to find the flavor profile you like. Then empty the barrel and enjoy a cocktail in an ice-filled Collins glass, topped with a splash of cola. Add the Talisker Storm to the barrel and age for 1 month. Post on Instagram. Get nasty comments. Go off social media for a while.

THE EFF-ME-UP FINISHES

There was much confusion, if not mockery, in the fall of 2017 when a TTB filing revealed Nashville's Belle Meade had plans to release a bourbon aged in honey barrels. But wait a second, everyone said, since when is honey aged in barrels? I even added to the Twitter clowning by noting, "Maybe they're just aging it in those honey *bottles* that look like fat bears."

For the record, the TruBee Honey company does actually make a cask-aged honey. Still, all the goofing around had given me an idea.

While things like honey and maple syrup are perhaps too sticky to add to your own mini barrel without ruining it, I wondered, what if you simply took a bottle of honey you had already gone through and used that as a finishing vessel? Let's be honest, it's impossible to ever fully finish a bottle of honey, as residue perma-lingers on the bottle's walls; perhaps it would add some interesting notes to whiskey. From there, my mind started spinning with all sorts of other eff-me-up finishes I could do, using not barrels but the bottles the following products actually come in.

HONEY

It will produce a honey liqueur far less artificial-tasting and far more appealing (especially in texture) than the "flavored" products a few major distilleries have on the market because their shareholders make them.

MAPLE SYRUP

Inspired by New York's Tuthilltown Spirits, which actually does age its Hudson Maple Cask Rye in whiskey barrels that had formerly held Wood's Syrup. Take a nearly empty bottle of real Grade A dark or even Grade B maple syrup (not that Aunt Jemima or Mrs. Butterworth's crap) and throw some spicy rye whiskey in it.

TABASCO

Most people probably don't realize that Tabasco is actually white oak barrel-aged before bottling. Those slight wood notes pair surprisingly well with a sweeter bourbon. Likewise, the actual Tabasco character integrates better than you'd expect, making for an oily whiskey with a now peppery nose, smoky body, and slightly acidic, stinging finish that is kinda fun. The tiny Tabasco bottle also means you don't have to waste much whiskey on this experiment. (And right after I wrote this section, George Dickel announced plans to release a Tabasco barrel-finished product!)

SOY SAUCE

If the first three eff-me-ups made at least some sense, this seems guaranteed to be ruinous to a whiskey. Not so. Many older, higher-proof scotches often have a bit of a soy sauce note, and, bolstered by actual soy sauce, the result is a savory whiskey that works nicely on its own or in a meatier cocktail like a Bloody Mary. Just don't use those little plastic packets you get with your sushi delivery.

FISH SAUCE

Now you think I'm surely screwing with you. But again, some seaside scotch distilleries produce quite briny drams, sometimes even said to have an almost "fishy" taste. Whatever the case, this will seriously up the umami notes in your scotch. Even better if you use a barrel-aged fish sauce like the terrific one from Michigan's BLiS. Go for it. You know you want to.

LEATHER BAG FINISHING

Forget tiny barrels, tiny bottles, and even honey bears. The most avant-garde way to age whiskey these days is in a damn leather bag. No, you can't just pull out that fake Louis Vuitton duffel you bought on Canal Street. Instead, you're going to want a goatskin bota bag, a traditional Spanish wine canteen that kind of looks like something a LARPer would carry to a medieval faire. (They run anywhere from $10 to $200, depending on quality.) It's not quite as weird an aging vessel as it sounds. Many whiskeys already have a hint of leather in them, and this just amps that up a bit, drying out the sweeter caramel notes, rounding out the bitterness, while adding an oily texture. Bars like London's Artesian and Las Vegas's Bazaar Meat have made leather bag cocktails for a few years, some even using a solera method, constantly refilling the bag so it's never completely empty. Now you, too, can be the weirdo offering guests a pour from your leather goat sack of booze.

LUKE SCHMUECKER'S

VERMONT CIDER FINISHING

Luke Schmuecker isn't just a good friend and drinking buddy; he has his talons in many aspects of the alcohol industry. He's a connoisseur of Pét-Nat wine, a cofounder of the Beer Exchange, and a partner in Shacksbury Cider, one of the country's most interesting cider producers. He manages to use that last love for an intriguing home barrel finish, which he matches with whiskey from next-door Vermont neighbor WhistlePig. (True to form, if you Google Map from cofounder Colin Davis's barn—where Shacksbury was first fermented—to WhistlePig Farm, it notes "This route includes roads that are closed in winter.") The result is a rye whiskey that still has a dry spice but is slightly more rounded with a great "apple cellar" nose and caramelized sugar body.

1 LITER SHACKSBURY DRY

1 LITER WHISTLEPIG 10 YEAR

Fill your barrel with the Shacksbury Dry and cover your bunghole with either an air lock or cheesecloth. As the cider is bottle conditioned, little bubbles will want to escape, and a blow-off is possible. Empty the barrel after two weeks and retain the cider. Fill the barrel with rye whiskey. Taste daily starting on day 7, monitoring until you are pleased with the flavor profile. Feel free to test with other styles of whiskey and other varieties of cider.

VERTS MONTS

MAKES 1 COCKTAIL

Schmuecker's house cocktail expands the Vermont theme to one focused on alpine ingredients that he describes as having an "alpine forest" flavor. The Génépi is made with Alpine herbs, while Chambéry is in Savoie, pretty much the Vermont of France if we're being honest.

Pair this cocktail with a huge bowl of mussels that have been cooked in a broth made from your oak-aged cider, Dijon mustard, crème fraîche, and shallots.

1½ OUNCES SHACKSBURY-FINISHED WHISTLEPIG 10 YEAR (RECIPE PRECEDES)

¾ OUNCE DOLIN VERMOUTH DE CHAMBÉRY DRY

¾ OUNCE DOLIN GÉNÉPI

LEMON TWIST, FOR GARNISH

Pour the ingredients into a mixing glass with ice and stir until chilled. Strain into a rocks glass with a giant ice cube in it. Express the lemon twist over the drink and use as a garnish.

THE SODA TRIALS

Most all drinkers, including me, first dipped our toes into the wonderful world of whiskey courtesy of a Jack and Coke (or Beam and Coke or a Crown and Coke or . . . you get the point). Of course, no respectable whiskey geek would dare drink a whiskey and Coke (for shame!). Still, you can't deny it's a killer combo. So why not just finish with Coke? And try some other sodas as well. For each finish, fill the barrel for a day with the following sodas, being careful that the carbonation doesn't cause overflows.

COKEHEAD

Use Mexican Coke if possible as its real cane sugar does a better job of flavoring the wood than the corn syrup crap. (Plus, it won't give you dementia.) Regular Old No. 7 Jack is fine, but the pricier Single Barrel is preferred. Carefully monitor your whiskey from day one, as it can quickly start picking up vinegary notes.

DR (JAMES E.) PEPPER

While I don't really know anyone who drinks a whiskey and Dr Pepper, maybe we should. Those dark fruit (some say prune) notes in the beverage combine and contrast beautifully with many flavors inherent in bourbon—everything from the caramel notes of Eagle Rare, to the chocolaty parts of James E.

Pepper, to the vanilla bomb that is Elmer T. Lee, making finishing the latter taste like a dollop of cherry-drizzled vanilla ice cream. Again, look for the cane sugar–based Dr Pepper that comes out of some plants in Texas.

THE MOUNTAIN AMBLER

Beloved by West Virginians, who drink so much of it their teeth fall out courtesy of an infliction called "Mountain Dew mouth" (please don't Google Image that), it's only apt we'd use a West Virginia whiskey as well. Smooth Ambler's Old Scout American Whiskey is able to calm down the insane sweetness in  the Dew. A sharp rye whiskey or even Islay scotch also works surprisingly well. Add a few ounces of Green Chartreuse to the barrel to bolster the herbal notes.

CREAMED CORN

Root beer and bourbon seem like a silly combination . . . but there I was on a tour at Buffalo Trace being served its Bourbon Cream with a splash of root beer, producing an almost root beer float–like sensation. Either season the barrel with root beer and add Bourbon Cream or season the barrel with cream soda and add Buffalo Trace. Both work nicely.

CHAPTER 5

SMOKING

TAKE THE BATTERIES OUT OF THE DETECTORS

Man has always known fire wasn't just important for the continuing progress of civilization; it's really cool too. Likewise, one of the flashiest ways you can play with your whiskey is by smoking it.

I know what you're thinking. Many scotches are *already* smoky. So why waste energy, money, time, and pyromaniacal tendencies doing it yourself? Well . . . because scotch whisky is only peat smoked. And there's a whole gigantic world of wood and other flammable flavor ingredients out there that we can fire-inject into our favorite brown waters.

I've been particularly inspired by Whiskey Del Bac Dorado, a mesquite wood–smoked whiskey made by Hamilton Distillers in Tucson, Arizona. The product tastes like a bag of alcoholic barbecue Lay's potato chips, and I think that's a good thing. The idea for that product started not from a whiskey maker but from furniture artisans. Stephen Paul and his daughter Amanda ran the boutique Arroyo Design, where they produced high-end chairs, tables, and armoires made of mesquite wood from the nearby Sonoran Desert. While  barbecuing with mesquite scraps and drinking scotch one day, the Pauls got the nutty idea to make their own whiskey using malted barley that had been dried, not by peat smoke, but by mesquite fire.

For demonstrating such ingenuity, the Pauls are heroes in my book (in *this* book) and Whiskey Del Bac has swept up awards in the ensuing years. We can try to follow their lead in our own whiskey lives.

The world is your oyster when you start adding smokes to whiskeys, and it's a whole lot easier than you'd think. (You're *not* going to have to learn to malt barley like the Pauls did.) Best of all, the smoke often smooths away a lot of harsh notes, especially those inherent in "young" craft whiskey. Hate that overly oaky, grainy two-year-old product you just bought for $50 from your neighbor who just started distilling? Don't toss that stuff down the drain. Smoke it.

Of course, adding intriguing smokes that the big boys would never use can also elevate bourbons, ryes, and scotches to crazy complex levels.

In the following pages, we will look at methods for infusing whiskey with smokes of various flavor, as well as a few more exotic examples currently being produced by professional bartenders, chefs, and distillers.

STEVEN RAICHLEN

—

Born in Japan, raised in Baltimore, and, not to mention, a Fulbright Scholar with a degree in French literature, Raichlen might seem an unlikely barbecue connoisseur. In actuality, the Cordon Bleu–trained chef is an expert on the art of grilling and smoking, with some two dozen books on the subject. The five-time James Beard Award winner's 2016 book *Project Smoke* is a collection of recipes for how to smoke everything from meats to veggies to desserts to even . . . alcohol. In his own words on the subject of smoking . . .

You can literally smoke anything. Of course, some things make more sense than others.

If you think about it, wood is such an important component of so many whiskeys. That's why it makes complete sense to bring smoke, wood, and whiskey together. And, of course, as we all know, there's one family of whiskeys that *is* already smoked. That's Islay whisky from Scotland, where the barley is dried over peat. I've even smoked meat with peat, although it's illegal to bring peat back to the United States. (How the heck did I get some? Oh yeah, an Irish company sold me some chunks and lumps. I didn't feel it worked as well or was as interesting as wood, though.)

I approach combining woods and alcohols less from a flavor profile and more from a geography point of view. So, if I'm smoking a mezcal or tequila, I'm inclined to use mesquite. That's the natural wood of that part of Mexico. If I was doing applejack or brandy or calvados, I'd probably use applewood. When it comes to whiskey, I most often use oak, because of the association with the bourbon barrels.

The Smoking Gun Pro (a handheld smoker) is one of my favorite smokers. I have many of them and use them all the time. The beauty of it is you can use it to do a test run of the same drink with a different, odd kind of wood for each glass. See which one works best and go with that.

My experience, though, is that the flavor differences in wood are pretty subtle when combined with whiskey.

I built an old-fashioned smokehouse at my place in Martha's Vineyard while I was writing *Project Smoke*. I smoked about 30 different things in it, including cocktails. If you don't have a smokehouse or Smoking Gun, another easy way to smoke whiskey is to pour it in an aluminum foil pan and put that over another pan of ice. Now you can put it in a grill or a water smoker or even an offset barrel smoker. (When you're smoking whiskey, you want to keep it cold. It can't get too hot or it becomes volatilized.)

Another technique that I highlight in *Project Smoke* is smoking just the glass instead of smoking the spirit. That's a much easier way to test things out. I use that method for a cocktail I call Dragon's Breath. What you do with that is you smoke a big brandy snifter, really coat the inside of the glass, then turn it upside down and set it on a coaster. If you're quick about it, when you take it off the coaster and fill the glass, the smoke will hopefully still be coming out. That's pretty cool.

I also smoke ice cubes, believe it or not. That works too, and you can pour a whiskey or a cocktail over them. When I first did it, the ice would melt when I smoked it, and then I'd refreeze them. Then, in a "duh" moment, I realized, "Why not just smoke the water and freeze it?"

There's really no wrong way to smoke whiskey.

HOW TO SMOKE WHISKEY

When it comes to smoking whiskey, no method is necessarily "best." It all depends on what kindling you are utilizing, smoke intensity you'd like to add, disposable income, and general methods you prefer. (And also what is least likely to cause the fire department to arrive and your landlord to keep your security deposit.) Here are the most popular options.

● ●

THE SMOKING GUN METHOD

You'll Need: The Smoking Gun Pro

Best for use at bars or apartments without outdoor access, Breville PolyScience's Smoking Gun device is able to inject smoky flavors without any heat. Originally designed to add a finishing touch of smoke to meats and vegetables, it was quickly adapted by bartenders for cocktails and spirits. I first saw it in use at Manhattan's swank spirits restaurant Fine & Rare. For home use, simply snake the handheld gun's rubber tube into a half-empty whiskey bottle, inject the smoke, and cap the bottle. Give it a little shake and allow the smoke to infuse for a few seconds to a few minutes. The easiest, safest, and most portable of any of these methods, the device can be found for $100 to $150 at luxury kitchen stores and on Amazon. If you are unable to find one, or dislike the Smoking Gun, the Aladdin Smoker works in a similar manner, although it is a tad more expensive.

THE SMOKING BOX METHOD

You'll Need: A cedar box or special smoking box (and a smoking gun)

As opposed to adding cold smoke straight to the bottle, a smoking box will

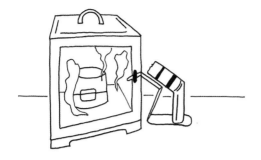

allow for smoke to surround the whiskey (or cocktail) but not get as fully infused directly into it. This is good for a light, seasoning smoke, one mainly aromatic. A full bottle will not fit inside most boxes, so this method is also best for single-serving smokes. The Smoking Box from Crafthouse by Fortessa is specifically designed for alcohol smoking, having been designed by acclaimed bartender Charles Joly. At around $250, it comes with its own smoking gun.

THE FISHBOWL METHOD

You'll Need: A culinary torch and a glass cloche

This method is similar to the smoking box in how the smoke infuses the alcohol; the one difference is in how the smoke is created. Atop a nonflammable surface, build a small campfire of kindling out of the particular wood or other ingredient you wish to smoke. You can sprinkle the wood with the whiskey to make it a little more flammable before starting your fire. (If you don't have a culinary torch, a lighter should work as well.) Once a fire is going, cover it as well as your tumbler or pan of whiskey with a glass cloche, which looks a little like one of those cake covers at a diner or even an upside-down fishbowl. This method is used at places like Seattle's Canon: Whiskey and Bitters Emporium, one of the finest whiskey bars in the world.

THE BARBECUE SMOKER METHOD

You'll Need: An outdoor smoker

This method can be used with pretty much any outdoor smoker or grill, from a $30 Weber up to those $5,000 Lang models that have a trailer hitch and

that your crazy uncle drives to brisket contests every weekend. Fill a hotel pan or Pyrex baking dish with whiskey to create a large surface area of exposure. Use your wood source as kindling in the same way you would for meats. Keep your pan away from the flame with the grill hood closed. After a few minutes of smoking, depending on desired intensity, funnel the whiskey back into bottles.

THE COLD SMOKER METHOD

You'll Need: A cold smoker

If you have a homemade cold smoker at your home, you probably don't need my advice on how to smoke anything. Must be nice to have one. Can I come over sometime? I'll bring beer.

• •

COMMON SMOKES

The following are a few of the more common culinary woods that people use for smoking. You can buy most of these woods online, or you can just take them from that particular tree. When using them, play with smoking "in" and "around" the whiskey until you get your desired flavor profile and intensity. For nonwoods, a smoking gun is typically the best device to use.

ALDER

Best with: PNW single malts like those from Westland and House Spirits
This musky smoke adds a certain "Pacific Northwest" forest note to whiskey. Fittingly, it's good for the emerging single malts of that region.

BEECH

Best with: Anything
The same wood the so-called "King of Beers," Budweiser, is filtered through, beechwood smoking whiskey adds a faint dusting of flavor, akin to a poor man's oak.

HICKORY

Best with: Tennessee whiskey
Perhaps the most common barbecue smoke source, it adds a nice bacon note to the whiskey. (Although a man they call the Peg Leg Porker [see page 148] questions whether you should ever smoke a whiskey with hickory.)

MAPLE

Best with: Rye
A mild smoke that adds a nice kiss of sugary sweetness. Good for adding a touch of flavor to more one-note, spicy ryes.

OAK

Best with: Anything

This full-flavored wood is what the vast majority of whiskey barrels are made from. Thus it pretty much works well with *all* whiskeys, adding a heavy smoke flavor but not much additional complexity or aftertaste.

OLIVE

Best with: Asian whiskeys

A lighter version of mesquite, its sweet, earthy flavors work best with more delicate whiskeys, like those single malts coming out of Japan, Taiwan, and India.

MESQUITE

Best with: Young American craft whiskeys, corn whiskeys

One of the hottest-burning woods, it imparts a strong and earthy flavor, one reminiscent of barbecue Lay's potato chips if you ask me.

FRUIT WOODS (CHERRY, APPLE, GRAPE, PEACH, PEAR, ETC.)

Best with: Rye whiskey

Distinctly sweet and pleasant, although often faint, fruit woods will appeal to people who claim not to like smoke. As these people might also not like the spiciness of a rye whiskey, it's a match made in your smoking gun.

CITRUS WOODS (LEMON, ORANGE, ETC.)

Best with: Lightly peated scotch, Irish whiskey

These woods are intense and

should be used sparingly. They each impart an oily, tropical aroma to whiskey. Some people think citrus wood smoking can make a whiskey taste almost like an aged gin.

NUT WOODS (ALMOND, MACADAMIA, WALNUT, PECAN, ETC.)

Best with: High-proof bourbon

These woods are intense and distinctive in their nutty flavor, although they can sometimes add a hint of bitterness on the finish. They work best with more robust whiskeys, especially barrel-proof bourbons. Feel free to also play around with these various nuts' shells as a smoking source.

EXOTIC SMOKES

The following are nonwoods that can also create fun smokes, although these are also more likely to create potential disasters. Best advised to try the following in smaller batches and/or at someone else's apartment.

DRIED COCONUT

Best with: Bourbon

It adds a toasted coconut note that bolsters many of the same notes inherent in American whiskeys after oak aging. Feel free to try smoking other dried fruits as well.

JUNIPER BERRIES

Best with: Herbaceous ryes

Smoking the featured botanical in gin adds a brilliant, piney aroma that is utterly distinct. Some people use juniper wood as well, but be sure to note that all conifer woods can emit a potentially poisonous substance.

CINNAMON STICKS

Best with: Anything

There are few more pleasant odors than that of smoking cinnamon sticks. It injects a wintry, dessert-like aroma into any whiskey.

ALLSPICE BERRIES

Best with: Anything

Aromatic and spicy (of course), allspice berries add a Jamaican rum–like tinge to any whiskey they touch. They also work terrifically in partnership with cinnamon sticks, which round out the flavor into one perfectly suited for cold weather.

DRIED HERBS (BASIL, ROSEMARY, THYME, OREGANO, ETC.)

Best with: Blended scotch, Irish whiskey

Play around with single herbs and blends to add a zestiness and herbaceousness to milder whiskeys. They work especially well with more savory, "meaty" scotches.

DRIED FLOWERS (LAVENDER, LILAC, ETC.)

Best with: Speyside scotch

The lovely floral notes added by smoking dried flowers can easily be overwhelmed by too spicy or caramel-heavy whiskeys. These smokes play best with vanilla-heavy bourbons and scotches.

PINE/SPRUCE NEEDLES

Best with: Maybe . . . nothing?

While the idea of smoking some conifers for a nice alpine addition seems pretty cool, it is believed it could introduce toxins into the air and your alcohol. Not necessarily advised unless you're also the kind of person who freely drinks out of lead decanters.

SMOKED MINT JULEP

MAKES 1 COCKTAIL

The best way to get your ears wet in smoking whiskey is to start with a relatively basic cocktail. Steven Reichlen suggests trying with a Mint Julep, a drink he calls "America's most underappreciated cocktail—revered in Kentucky, consumed just about nowhere else." He thinks smoking the julep is just what's needed to rehabilitate the image of a beverage synonymous with the Kentucky Derby, but ignored the other 364 days of the year. His recipe creates an umami-heavy bourbon drink, perfect for making in bigger batches for large groups.

2 OUNCES BOURBON OF YOUR CHOICE

½ OUNCE SMOKED MINT SIMPLE SYRUP (RECIPE BELOW)

FRESH MINT SPRIGS, FOR GARNISH

CONFECTIONERS' SUGAR, FOR DUSTING

Fill a silver tumbler or bar glass three-quarters full with shaved or crushed ice. Add the bourbon and mint syrup. Stir briskly, then add more ice to the top. Dust the mint sprigs with confectioners' sugar and use as a garnish.

SMOKED MINT SIMPLE SYRUP

Makes 8 ounces

½ cup sugar

½ cup water

8 fresh mint leaves

Hickory chips

In a saucepan, combine the sugar, water, and mint and bring to a boil. Cook until the sugar has dissolved. Let the mixture cool to room temperature. Cover the saucepan with plastic wrap. Load a smoking gun with hickory chips, insert the hose under the plastic wrap, and fill the saucepan with hickory smoke. Let stand for 4 minutes, then stir the syrup. Re-cover with plastic and re-smoke. Repeat until you achieve the smoke flavor you like. Strain the syrup into a clean jar and store in the refrigerator until ready to use.

FIG WOOD-SMOKED PEACH GOMME SYRUP

If writing this book taught me anything, it's that there's a lot more wood on Earth than I had previously realized. While we've all heard of hickory and mesquite and maybe even applewood, it only makes sense that if some unique fruit grows on a tree, it probably also has its own unique wood type. Even still, and even if I knew figs grew on trees, I hadn't ever considered the existence of fig wood until I was introduced to it by Stephanie Andrews, the Jean Banchet Award winner as Chicago's best mixologist.

To be fair, she had only recently been in the same boat I was in. The bar manager at Billy Sunday, an amaro-focused cocktail bar in Chicago, she was at an event on a farm when her culinary director ran out of wood. Scrambling for ideas, he found fig trees on the property and quickly used their wood to cook some pork. "Whoa! What is this smell?" thought Andrews. "It just imparted this really awesome, unique flavor," she tells me. She knew she would have to take some back to the bar—and already had a perfect whiskey pairing for it in mind.

At the time, Andrews had been playing around with High West Silver Western Oat, an unaged moonshine, yes, but not one she found hot and flavorless. In fact, she thought the oats produced a pleasant stone fruit–like quality. A trip to the farmers' market led her to some peaches, which she smoked over the fig wood, creating a toasted coconuty flavor profile. Turning that into a peach gomme syrup, she now had the base for a perfect autumnal whiskey sour–like cocktail.

2 PEACHES, HALVED AND PITTED

12 OUNCES GOMME SYRUP

Place the peaches cut side down on the grill. Using fig wood as kindling, smoke with high direct heat for 2 to 3 minutes. Remove from the smoker and, while the fig wood–smoked peaches are still warm, dice them. Let them steep in a store-bought or homemade gomme syrup for 36 hours. Strain and then bottle for use in cocktails.

PAPA DON'T PREACH

MAKES 1 COCKTAIL

Upon finding a few boxes of Russian nesting dolls in the bar's basement, Andrews realized they would be perfect drink vessels for her new cocktail. First, though, her crew hand-painted over the Russian images with the visage of Billy Sunday, the temperance-touting evangelist the bar is named after (and now you get the cocktail's name). The obscure-to-most German Aromatique and Amaro Sibilla add seasonal spices and nutty notes. This quickly became one of the most acclaimed cocktails from Andrews.

1 ½ OUNCES HIGH WEST SILVER WESTERN OAT

1 OUNCE FIG WOOD–SMOKED PEACH GOMME SYRUP (RECIPE PRECEDES)

½ OUNCE TH. KRAMERS AROMATIQUE

¼ OUNCE AMARO SIBILLA

¾ OUNCE FRESH LEMON JUICE

1 EGG WHITE

5 DASHES ABBOTT'S AROMATIC AGED COCKTAIL BITTERS

Pour the whiskey, syrup, Aromatique, amaro, lemon juice, and egg white into a shaker without ice and dry shake. Add ice and shake again. Strain with a Hawthorne strainer into a small rocks glass and add the bitters to the top of the cocktail. Place into a Russian nesting doll. Smoke the insides of the doll with a smoking gun filled with grated fig wood and close it. The thick egg white traps the smoke aroma quite a bit. At Billy Sunday, bartenders open the doll upon presenting it to the customer.

VOLCANO VAPORIZED WEED WHISKEY

The Volcano is a vapor infuser, or vaporizer. Creating heat below the combustion point, it can take the oils out of ingredients and create vapors that you can, say, *inhale*, because nothing inside it ever burns.

Totally legitimate bars have started using them in their totally legitimate drinks, like the Aviary, which fires up a Volcano to add the scent of everything bagels to its rye whiskey and coffee cocktail named, *wink*, Wake and Bake. Of course you can also vaporize herbs like lemongrass and thyme, or you can just use, hehe, *herb*. Which is the one reason most people own the $600 device in the first place.

One such marijuana fan, who just so happens to also be a prominent mixologist in the Pacific Northwest, got the most obvious idea while drunk and stoned one night. She would use her Volcano to infuse weed into the half-empty whiskey bottle sitting on the coffee table.

Marijuana is actually a fairly tricky thing to infuse. It needs to be heated for the psychoactive THC to get activated. That's what makes the Volcano such a great device. Of course federal law prohibits—even in weed-legal states, like where our weed whiskey creator lives—selling marijuana in bars and selling alcohol in dispensaries. Thus the reason she would rather keep her infamy to herself.

½ GRAM FINELY GROUND CANNABIS (SATIVA STRAINS ARE RECOMMENDED FOR DAYTIME USE, INDICA STRAINS FOR NIGHT)

ONE 750-MILLILITER BOTTLE BARRELL BOURBON (OR ANY BOTTLE OF WHISKEY)

Similar to the smoking gun, the Volcano has a tiny bowl-like canister for filling with ingredients. Set the Volcano for your desired range between 370°F and 410°F and pack the chamber with cannabis. Add the Volcano's "mixology attachment" or a simple PVC tube from Home Depot. Turn the fan on and snake the other end of the tube into the bottle and into the whiskey itself. It will start gurgling with bubbles like a bong. Infuse for at least 30 seconds, let the liquid rest for a few seconds after that, then taste. Repeat the process, using more cannabis if necessary, until the desired flavor profile is reached. This can also be done, perhaps even more effectively, on single-serving pours.

THE MEZZROLE COCKTAIL

MAKES 1 COCKTAIL

A fan of New York's Jazz Era, Warren Bobrow named this drink after one hep cat called Mezz Mezzrow. Although he played clarinet with the likes of Louis Armstrong and Sidney Bechet, he was more well known for being the principal dealer of Mexican weed among the musicians of 1930s Harlem. There a "Mezzrole" became slang for some reefer. (You may notice this calls for a scant ¾ ounce of alcohol, yet Bobrow notes it is plenty potent at around 100 micrograms of THC per drink.)

2 OR 3 LUXARDO CHERRIES

½ OUNCE CANNABIS-INFUSED BARRELL BOURBON (TECHNIQUE PRECEDES)

¼ OUNCE CANNABIS-INFUSED UNCOUTH VERMOUTH SEASONAL WILDFLOWER BLEND

DASH OF AROMATIC BITTERS

DASH OF PEYCHAUD'S BITTERS

PINCH OF HIMALAYAN SALT

Muddle the Luxardo cherries in a cocktail glass. Pour the bourbon and vermouth into a mixing glass with ice and stir until chilled. Strain the alcohol into a cocktail glass over crushed ice, then dot with bitters to taste. Add a pinch of Himalayan salt and serve.

OTHER WAYS TO MAKE WEED WHISKEY

Bobrow, who authored *Cannabis Cocktails, Mocktails & Tonics: The Art of Spirited Drinks and Buzz-Worthy Libations* in 2016, prefers less flashy ways to infuse THC into his spirits. "I was looking for a nonantagonistic method," he told me, noting he lives in the Jersey suburbs. "I can medicate, and no one knows my business." For the following methods, since no heating goes on, you will need to "decarb" the marijuana first so it actually works. Bobrow uses a NOVA Decarboxylator by Ardent, but a microwave will do in a pinch—both create hardly any scent to alert those nosy neighbors. Bobrow uses around 14 grams per 750-milliliter bottle but admits that might be a tad much for most.

- Rapid Infusion, using an iSi Gourmet Whip (see page 161). Bobrow calls it "violent and exciting."

- The Magical Butter MB2E Machine, an herbal infuser. Two hours at 160°F, then top off with the whiskey.

- Double Broiler Method, where you add the whiskey and weed to the top half of a double boiler and let it infuse over a couple of hours while the water simmers slowly below. Just be sure your alcohol never boils itself and do not do this using a gas burner! This is a commonly used method, but also one of the more dangerous ones. Proceed at your own risk.

BRAHM CALLAHAN'S

CIGAR-SMOKED BUFFALO

Brahm Callahan grew up working on his family-run tobacco farm in western Massachusetts. Now a master sommelier and the beverage director for a series of fancy, alcohol-focused restaurants in Boston, he wanted to figure out a way to incorporate his lifelong love of cigars into cocktails (especially after the statewide smoking ban hit in 2004). Using the restaurant's convection smoker—a Weber Grill or even your oven will also work—he lightly smokes a cigar until its flavors infuse into the bourbon. Not to worry, no nicotine is transferred into the whiskey. Besides, scientists have found alcohol marinades kill smoker-created carcinogens. So, if you're essentially drinking the alcohol marinade itself, I'm sure you're golden.

SIX 750-MILLILITER BOTTLES BUFFALO TRACE BOURBON
1 MONTECRISTO NO. 2 CIGAR

Empty the bottles of bourbon into a hotel pan to create a large surface area. Place on the grill rack. Soak the cigar in water so it will not burn. Cut the cigar into small pieces and use as your kindling (where you'd typically place the wood or charcoals). Smoke for 20 minutes with a closed top. (You can adjust the ratios of cigar, bourbon, and smoke time, depending on what cigar-smoke level you find you like. Of note, a Montecristo is a milder cigar.) Funnel back into the bottles.

DEATH & TAXES

MAKES 1 COCKTAIL

Callahan designed the best-selling cocktail at steakhouse spot Grill 23 to calm down the intensity of the cigar, explaining, "I didn't want the smoke to be overpowering; I just wanted it to be on the finish." Folding the cigar-smoked bourbon into the herbaceous Fernet and sweet peach puree does the trick, mellowing out the cocktail quite a bit. It's a stiff drink but still subtle in flavor.

SPLASH OF FERNET-BRANCA, FOR RINSING

3 OUNCES CIGAR-SMOKED BUFFALO TRACE (RECIPE PRECEDES)

½ OUNCE FRESH LEMON JUICE

½ OUNCE PEACH SYRUP (PUREE FRESH PEACHES IN A FOOD PROCESSOR; MAKE THE SYRUP BY HEATING UP EQUAL AMOUNTS OF THE PUREE, WATER, AND SUGAR; LET IT COOL BEFORE STRAINING)

Rinse a cocktail glass with the Fernet-Branca and pour it out. Pour all the remaining ingredients into a shaker with ice and shake until chilled. Strain into the cocktail glass. Write it off on your tax return.

ZACHARY DAVIS'S

SMOKING THE BARREL TOO

A new oak barrel isn't just what holds American whiskey; it's what gives it most of its flavor too. But what if you could literally drink the entire barrel—liquid, wood, char, and all? Zachary Davis, as beverage director for Chef Michael Schulson's Philadelphia-area restaurants, came up with this exact idea back in 2015. Inspired by plank-smoked cocktails, Davis began fooling around with smoking used bourbon barrel staves he had purchased on Etsy of all places.

THE DOUBLE KNOT

MAKES 1 COCKTAIL

While bourbon barrel–smoking a bourbon might seem redundant if not pure overkill, Davis uses the process for this highly aromatic, autumn-by-the-fireplace sipper. This doubled-up Perfect Manhattan variant was first served as the signature cocktail at its namesake's multipurpose space. The complex cocktail manages to be sweet, spicy, and bitter, all in one.

CHOPPED BOURBON BARREL STAVE

CLOVES

CINNAMON STICKS, CRACKED

1 OUNCE MAKER'S 46

1 OUNCE GEORGE DICKEL RYE WHISKY

½ OUNCE PUNT E MES

½ OUNCE CARPANO BIANCO VERMOUTH

2 DASHES ANGOSTURA BITTERS

2 DASHES FEE BROTHERS ORANGE BITTERS

On a flat piece of bourbon barrel stave, or other flat fireproof surface, make a small campfire of a chopped-up stave with cloves and cracked cinnamon sticks atop it. Light it on fire with a culinary torch. Place a bulbous snifter glass over the fire and allow the smoke to coat the insides while you build the cocktail. Pour all the liquid ingredients into a mixing glass with ice and stir until chilled. Remove the snifter from the campfire and immediately strain the cocktail into the glass.

TEA-SMOKED SCOTCH

As already mentioned, wood isn't the only thing you can use to smoke whiskey. Fact is, anything small, combustible, and food grade will generally work. Loose-leaf teas are a terrifically cheap and easy way to add complex herbal notes to any whiskey. Lapsang souchong in particular works wonders. It's a Chinese style of tea that is dried over pinewood fire, giving it an already smoky flavor. While it works well with adding smoky notes to sweeter bourbons, I love to amp up already smoky scotches with it.

LOOSE-LEAF LAPSANG SOUCHONG TEA

ONE 750-MILLILITER BOTTLE LAPHROAIG QUARTER CASK, EMPTIED HALFWAY

Load a smoking gun with tea and insert the hose into the bottle, filling with smoke for 30 seconds. Cap and let stand for 4 minutes. Shake and then uncap. Repeat until you have reached a desired flavor profile. You can also simply smoke a single serving of the scotch if you do not wish to use a full bottle.

THE HOT SCOTCHY

MAKES 1 COCKTAIL

A basic hot toddy variant made by swapping in Scottish ingredients.

2 OUNCES LAPSANG-SMOKED LAPHROAIG (TECHNIQUE PRECEDES)

JUICE OF ½ LEMON

½ OUNCE SCOTTISH HEATHER HONEY

HOT WATER

Pour the scotch, lemon juice, and honey into a thick mug. Stir together. Top with hot water to taste. Drink and feel revived like you will never be sick another day in your life.

PECHUGA BOURBON (AKA TURKEY-SMOKED TURKEY)

Whether craft producer or big boy brand, whiskey production has become almost a little too factory-bound. Other spirits aren't so glossy and shiny. Take mezcal, for example, which remains quite "artisanal" (gag) even as the top producers are likewise snatched up by international conglomerates. Even so, the most celebratory and, yes, freaking insane way of producing the spirit remains quite hand-crafted. Called *pechuga*, Spanish for "breast," it involves hanging a literal raw turkey or chicken breast inside the copper still along with seasonal fruits. Some people think the steamed chicken fat that gets into the distillate rounds out the smoky product, while others think it is nothing more than symbolic. Who knows? Whatever the case, pechuga mezcals are exceedingly rare commercially and quite pricey if and when you find one.

Why should the mezcal industry have all the fun?

As far as I know, there is no pechuga whiskey in existence, although Illinois's FEW Spirits did once hang Chicago deep-dish pizza inside its whiskey still. Close, but I needed some genuine pechuga whiskey. Now, I wasn't going to start illicitly distilling in the backyard I don't even have, so I decided to try a poor man's way of pechuga-izing some.

1 TURKEY BREAST (OR ANY MEAT YOU TRADITIONALLY SMOKE LOW AND SLOW, LIKE PORK BUTT, HAM, RIBS, OR BRISKET)

THREE 750-MILLILITER BOTTLES WILD TURKEY 101 BOURBON OR RYE

3 PEACHES, SLICED

Spatchcock a turkey and smoke it over the wood of your choice (pecan works nicely) at 225°F for around 12 minutes per pound. Empty the bottles of Wild Turkey into a hotel pan to create a large surface area. In the final 30 minutes of smoking the turkey, add the hotel pan to the smoker, next to it. If you have a rack above the turkey and Wild Turkey, add the peaches and any other seasonal fruits you like. Remove the whiskey from the smoker and freeze overnight. Fat-wash in the morning and enjoy alongside a cold turkey sandwich (see page 159 for fat-washing techniques).

HICKORY-FILTERED BOURBON

However, not everyone thinks smoking whiskey is a smart thing to do.

"I've never tasted a smoked beer or smoked whiskey that I liked. Or a smoked cocktail with that Smoking Gun—they're always bitter and acrid," Carey Bringle tells me. I'd typically make fun of a guy who also claims to dislike smoky scotch and mezcal, but Bringle isn't just any guy. He's a literal smoke expert. An award-winning competitive barbecue cook for over a decade, he's run his acclaimed Peg Leg Porker restaurant in Nashville since 2013. A bourbon lover as well, when he decided it was time to make his own product, Bringle knew it needed to be uniquely his.

"I understand smoke," he tells me matter-of-factly. "People don't understand that smoke is another ingredient like salt or pepper or even hot sauce. You have to use it in moderation. If you think you can just use smoke for smoke's sake, you'll get a nasty product."

Thus Bringle felt that actually *smoking* his whiskey or even adding smoked spirals to the barrels would have created a bad, overly smoky product. He had another idea. He cleverly sourced some well-aged bourbon (from what many people believe to be George Dickel), then dumped it from its barrel through some hickory charcoals he had burned down himself. Why hickory wood specifically? Because, Bringle claims, hickory is what makes Tennessee barbecue Tennessee barbecue.

The resulting product, Peg Leg Porker Tennessee Straight Bourbon, is utterly unique, with just a hint of smoke but no bitter or acrid flavors. It's far from the "liquid smoke" that Bringle loathes. The hickory adds rustic, woody, and sweet caramel notes, playing well with those flavors already in the base product. It quickly became a critical darling too, winning a Double Gold at the prestigious San Francisco World Spirits Competition.

Unfortunately, Peg Leg Porker is still a fairly limited release. So you might have to just make your own. Bringle gives you his blessing and even admits it's not too hard. "People criticize the different ways to chemically get an end product," he tells me. "But a great end product is a great end product. I don't give a shit how you got there!"

4-INCH PIECES HICKORY WOOD
ONE 750-MILLILITER BOTTLE TENNESSEE WHISKEY

Burn the hickory wood pieces until they are coals. Pile them on a mesh filter, which is placed on top of a Cambro. Pour your favorite Tennessee whiskey through the column of coal. Use a sock filter to eliminate impurities before rebottling. Bringle believes other woods would work just as well; he simply hasn't tried them because of his homegrown affinity for hickory. Other people even like to extra-age commercially bought whiskey in an airtight container with the coals for an added smokiness.

PULLED PORK OLD-FASHIONED

MAKES 1 COCKTAIL

Inspired by Shannon Ponche's Daiquiri al Pastor at Brooklyn's Leyenda, I wanted to see if I could Americanize the drink a bit. While Ponche fat-washes white rum with an actual roasted pork shoulder, I thought the hickory notes would be enough to simulate Tennessee's best barbecue dish.

2 OUNCES HICKORY-FILTERED BOURBON (RECIPE PRECEDES)

½ OUNCE COLESLAW SYRUP (MAKE A SYRUP BY HEATING UP EQUAL AMOUNTS OF PURPLE CABBAGE JUICE, WATER, AND TURBINADO SUGAR; LET IT COOL BEFORE STRAINING)

2 DASHES FEE BROTHERS MOLASSES BITTERS

1 DASH BITTER BASTARDS BLACK PEPPER BITTERS

ORANGE TWIST

PORK RIND, FOR GARNISH

Pour the bourbon, syrup, and bitters into a mixing glass with ice and stir until chilled. Strain into a rocks glass with a giant ice cube in it. Express the orange twist over the drink and discard. Garnish with a pork rind.

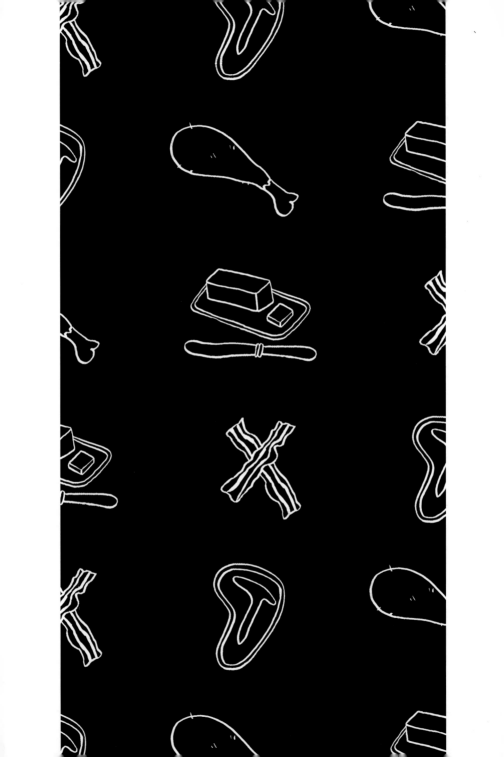

CHAPTER 6

FAT WASHING AND INFUSING

YOUR HOUSE WILL SOON LOOK LIKE A LABORATORY

Back when I was a young bozo struggling weekly to scrape together enough cash to get drunk and forget my failure of a life, I spent a lot of time at a bar called the Russian Vodka Room. Located just on the edge of Times Square before it transitioned into Hell's Kitchen where I lived, the small, windowless joint was like nothing I'd ever seen at the time. Pitch-black with a bar in the round, it was serviced by waiters who looked like KGB agents and blonde bombshell bartenders who looked like the mail-order brides of your dreams. There was live piano music. During happy hour, liter bottles of Baltika 4, a dark Russian lager, were just $2.50, while shots of the house vodkas were a mere buck. It wasn't just any vodka, though; set on shelves surrounding the bar were giant glass vats full of colorful liquids that spanned the rainbow, all with various . . . things floating in them.

Cranberries, cinnamon sticks, horseradish roots. These simple infusions supplied the $1 happy hour vodka that would have the details of my crummy week erased well before 9:00 p.m. struck every Friday night.

That was over a decade ago. In the intervening years I've gotten a little more successful at life. And while today the Russian Vodka Room apparently still exists according to Yelp (a recent review: "We loved [the] Soviet Union decor, place looks like Stalin's office"), I'm now into more . . . let's say, upscale infusions.

Whiskey is obviously the utter opposite of vodka, and for the most part you don't want to infuse your pricey whiskey by simply dumping some blueberries into the bottle. Since whiskey has such powerful, complex flavors, you're going to want to try to match it with equally bold, complex flavors. Like, say, *meat*. But, again, you don't just drop some ground round into a bottle of Jim Beam and call it a day.

If an alcohol "infusion" is what you did in college—merely dumping fresh fruit into a bottle and revisiting it a few days later—to infuse whiskey with more ambitious foodstuff you're going to need 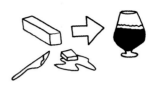 to learn a fairly tricky tactic called fat washing. First described in a 2007 *Food & Wine* article by Nick Fauchald, fat washing involves infusing an alcohol with a flavorful fat. Fat won't dissolve in most liquids, but it will dissolve in alcohol. Chilling that mixture until the fat resolidifies, then skimming it off, completes the fat wash. This is the only way to infuse a spirit with the flavors of, say, brown butter or hazelnuts or, yes, meat, without leaving any greasiness behind.

Fat washing would truly catapult to fame later in 2007, when PDT's Don Lee created his Benton's Old-Fashioned, a cocktail made with Four Roses bourbon that had been fat-washed with smoky Tennessee bacon. Even today it remains surely the greatest infused whiskey anyone has ever borne. In fact, it is still on PDT's menu over a decade later.

On the following pages are some ideas for fat washes along with simpler infusions that work best with whiskey, with recipes from bar industry professionals and some more *insane* ideas I've come up with myself. Even if you muck up a batch or two—don't worry, you won't—it's going to be a helluva lot more fun than having giant vats of vodka lining your kitchen shelves, fraying chunks of gross pineapple floating in them.

MEAGHAN MONTAGANO

—

Meaghan Montagano is a longtime fixture on the New York bartending scene. She's crafted cocktails at Extra Fancy, the Michelin-starred La Sirena, and most recently Casa Pública, a Mexico City–inspired bar and restaurant in Williamsburg, Brooklyn. She has long loved making intriguing fat washes and infusions, like her buttered corn "blue whiskey." In her own words on the subject of fat washing and infusions . . .

I'm usually eating anytime I get inspired. Or I have a random idea while grocery shopping. Or I think of the season we're in. Then it's going down a rabbit hole to try and figure out how to make that into a cocktail. It's like throwing spaghetti on a wall. Some infusions are god awful. But many work.

I love *The Flavor Bible* books, I swear by them; they're literally the best thing ever. Say, I think of doing something with pineapple, I just look up "pineapple" in the index and it tells me what flavors pair well with it. It's mainly meant for cooking, but every bar person uses it as a way to delve a little deeper into flavor profiles and combinations that work. It's a constant reference:

"Oh, what can I infuse with X? Or, can I infuse this base spirit with Y?"

I recommend using a full bottle for any infusion. You don't want to make too small a batch. You lose a lot in the process. Especially with fruits that suck up a lot of the alcohol.

I wouldn't necessarily infuse a really good whiskey, though. I wouldn't infuse, say . . . Hibiki. Look for $15 to $30 spirits. Buy a handle of the cheap stuff to practice with. *Hashtag college days.* Break the handle into six 10-ounce jars and start experimenting. You can figure out what you like that way, what works. You can get an idea of what flavors will be created, and then you can use a better whiskey from there.

A lot of regular folk, they really have no idea, and they get seduced by branding and marketing. You don't need to. You can always get two pretty good bottles for the price of one expensive bottle. Old Forester is great. So is Evan Williams Black or Green Label. Old Crow is good and very inexpensive. There's a lot of these cheap, easily accessible whiskeys. And now with two bottles you can mess around a lot more.

For figuring out ratios of ingredients you're infusing, it really comes down to what you're using. You need to be testing your infusion every single day—tasting it. Spicy stuff is the easiest to infuse. You get quick results. Quarter a pepper, leave the seeds in for spice. You'll have a spicy whiskey within an hour. Most fruits, things like cucumbers or strawberries or melon especially, they take a day. Something as delicate as lavender or thyme, that takes two weeks. You never know what will happen. I've done ginger and beet infusions. That one turned the liquor dark purple.

A fat wash is just a fancy infusion. It's just literally working with pure fat. Bacon fat is the best to infuse with. Butter is really great, too, and so readily available of course. You can fat wash with nuts. With peanut butter. If you have connections within the culinary world, you can probably get duck fat or something even weirder than that. There's always a way. Most people don't want to keep fat around the kitchen and are, in fact, scared of it. They'll gladly give it to you for free.

I wouldn't try to infuse, like, steak . . . or hot dogs. Other weird proteins like that. Things that are fragile or perish aren't usually very good. Frozen fruits are great. There's more water content behind them. Candy works. I do love grape Hubba Bubba and Jolly Ranchers. Twizzlers you can definitely do. Nerds, they're so small, they break down quicker.

Just get weird in your grocery store.

Think about your modifiers if you're going to use your infusion for making cocktails. You can go into the farmers' market and for $20 buy a ton of ingredients. Strange sugars and dried fruits and spices. What really gets ignored, and shouldn't, is that "ethnic" food aisle in, say, a suburban ShopRite. The Chinese, Spanish, or Mexican section, whatever. It'll have all those great dried peppers in bags that most people overlook. Test them out as a simple syrup first. It's cheaper, and you can be super experimental without wasting $20 on alcohol.

Use cheap white sugar—you know, the kind that is slowly killing us all—make a simple syrup, and toss some peppers or Mexican oregano in. If it doesn't taste good in a cocktail, you can use it to glaze a pork chop instead.

I call what I do with infusions "mom cooking." You're just guessing the amount that works. You're guessing a recipe. It's what feels right. Always start with fewer ingredients, and then you can always add more.

There's really no right or wrong with infusions. (Unless some fruit goes rancid.) When you have an idea, and there's no recipe online, just follow your gut. And if you do mess up an infusion? Just use it in a Jungle Juice punch. That's my motto in life. Just use it in a Jungle Juice.

HOW TO
FAT WASH

Fat washing is just a fancier way to infuse a spirit, in our case whiskey. Anything that has soluble fats can be fat washed, although the following technique will vary a little depending on what sort of ingredient you are trying to infuse.

∙∙∙

1. Choose the ingredient(s) you wish to infuse. Duck fat, hazelnut oil, Butterfingers . . . go wild! Of course you might not simply be able to buy, say, duck fat, in which case you'll have to render your own. In other words, cook a duck, and instead of tossing the grease left in the pan down the sink and pissing off your landlord when you clog up his pipes, use it for your fancy whiskey infusion.

2. Add liquefied fat (hot, if possible) to whiskey at around a ratio of one ounce per 750-milliliter bottle. If you can, do this in a Cambro container, which allows more surface area contact between the alcohol and the liquefied fat. Let the ingredients infuse for several hours at room temperature.

3. Afterward, put the entire Cambro in the freezer for as little as 12 hours but quite possibly for a couple days. It really depends. You're waiting as long as it takes for the oils from the fat to freeze and separate from the alcohol—because, remember, alcohol can't freeze. The alcohol left behind will be infused with the flavor of the fat, and the texture might be a tad thicker.

4. Once that is the case, skim the fat off the top, then strain the rest of the whiskey through a cheesecloth to eliminate all the solids still lingering behind.

5. Put the infused whiskey back into the original whiskey bottle—it will now lack a few ounces—and store for a few weeks up to a few months. Always store in the fridge, as there's the potential for funkiness festering due to heat and oxidation at room temperature.

• •

While most bartenders today are making fat wash–infused whiskeys with specific cocktails in mind, that is not a necessity. I mean, it's not that hard to figure out ways to employ a baconized bourbon. In the following pages we'll look at some favorite fat-washed whiskeys courtesy of professional barkeeps (along with the cocktails they work best in), as well as a few homers I've hit while fat washing and infusing myself.

ON RAPID INFUSIONS

Sometimes you may want to get fancy with fat but don't have 24 hours or more to see your genius realized. Carpe diem. It's time to seize the day and make this crazy infusion lickety split. No problem, so long as you have an iSi Gourmet

Whip, which runs less than $100. Yes, it's typically used in the culinary world for making whipped cream, but skilled bartenders of the past decade have also figured out a way to use it for ASAP infusions. Essentially, nitrous oxide (N2O) forces the alcohol into the ingredients before it is released out again, now containing the infusion.

1. Stuff the reservoir with your preferred flavoring ingredients, then pour the whiskey over the top. Screw on the top.

2. Screw in the N2O cartridge until the gas releases into the whipper. Let it stand for a minute. (Optional: Inhale some. Start laughing. Forget about stupid infusions.)

3. Remove the N2O and discard. Replace with another N2O cartridge and shake the canister for a minute or so.

4. Keeping the whipper upright so as not to lose any liquid, spray out the gas. A little liquid may accidentally eject, so use an empty glass to catch the spray.

5. Unscrew the whipper's top and pour the remaining liquid through a mesh strainer and into an empty bottle.

It's not all fun and infusions though. In 2017, a famed French fitness blogger died when a faulty whipped cream canister exploded and struck her chest.

BLUE WHISKEY

A Mexican restaurant is the last place you'd expect to find interesting stuff going on in the whiskey world, but perhaps you shouldn't—whiskey is less sacrosanct there and more apt to be screwed with. The idea for blue whiskey was created on the fly while Montagano browsed through the aisles of Kalustyan's, a specialty spice store in Manhattan that is popular among bartenders. She had recently been at Three Dots and a Dash in Chicago, where she admired one of Paul McGee's drinks that came with a banana dolphin garnish in it.

"I said, 'I don't care what is in that drink; I want that drink,'" she told me. So she became determined to re-create that visual sensation by making a blue drink that wasn't a Blue Hawaiian—you know, something artificially blue. She realized the dried Peruvian blue corn on Kalustyan's shelf might do the trick. The fact that she had just gotten a shipment of Hudson New York Corn Whiskey, an unaged spirit distilled from 100% corn, made a decision to commit "corn-on-corn crime" as she calls it, an obvious choice.

2 POUNDS DRIED PERUVIAN BLUE CORN

TWO 750-MILLILITER BOTTLES HUDSON NEW YORK CORN WHISKEY

2 POUNDS UNSALTED BUTTER

Roast the corn kernels on a baking sheet at 180°F for a few minutes just to bring out the aromas ("It's like making popcorn—pop the essence of it," Montagano explains). Dump the hot kernels into a sealable container holding whiskey from both bottles. Let sit for at least 1 day. At this point it will be a beautiful blue color but still taste like moonshine. Strain out the kernels and reserve them. With corn being so porous and absorbent, you will have only about 750 milliliters of liquid left. Put half of the corn in a really hot and completely flat skillet with no oil and retoast. Switch to low heat and add a pound of butter. Cook until fully melted and blue but not browned. Pour the butter (but not the corn kernels) back into the whiskey. Repeat the process with the other half of the corn. Stir together, seal, and put in the freezer overnight. The next day, once taken out of the freezer, immediately strain through a chinois (if you let it sit, you'll have solids stuck in the whiskey) and place back in the bottle. It may take a while to capture all the fat-washed whiskey, but once you do, you'll have a liquid with a texture that Montagano describes as "blue velvet." She cautions that you should wear gloves throughout the entire process, otherwise you'll end up with "Smurf hands."

YOU'RE MY BOY BLUE

MAKES 1 COCKTAIL

Montagano's "wild" variation on a Manhattan takes her blue whiskey and then adds sweet vermouth and a terroir-driven crème de cacao (made of Venezuelan cacao and Mexican vanilla) to further round out the drink. That also turns it more purplish. So labor intensive and expensive to produce, it was rarely on Casa Pública's menu, mainly existing as a cult favorite. The three-day process necessitates wasting half of your whiskey and thus creates a cocktail that Montagano had to price at $17 a pop.

1½ OUNCES BLUE WHISKEY (RECIPE PRECEDES)

¾ OUNCE CARPANO ANTICA FORMULA SWEET VERMOUTH

¼ OUNCE TEMPUS FUGIT CRÈME DE CACAO

2 DASHES MOLE BITTERS

2 DASHES ANGOSTURA BITTERS

LEMON TWIST, FOR GARNISH

Pour the whiskey, vermouth, and crème de cacao into a mixing glass with ice, add the bitters, and stir until chilled. Strain into a rocks glass with a giant ice cube in it. Express the lemon twist over the drink and use as a garnish. Order some tacos.

BENTON'S BACON FAT—INFUSED FOUR ROSES BOURBON

PDT originally got its Benton's bacon fat hand-delivered courtesy of David Chang's nearby Momofuku Ssäm Bar. You? You're going to have to render the bacon fat yourself. Please try to find some Benton's. I know, I know, I know . . . bacon is bacon. Even the $5-a-pound store brand generic stuff is pretty good—I like Oscar Mayer Thick Cut myself—but Benton's Hickory Smoked Country Bacon is actually worth shelling out for. It's no secret among foodies, who regularly write paeans to the Madisonville, Tennessee, product. It's expensive for bacon, but not *that* expensive. You can order it straight from the purveyor online or go to the absolute most high-end "larder" in your town and ask for it by name. The eyes of the guy behind the counter will light up . . . and then he'll promptly charge you $20 a pound. You won't regret it.

Bacon maestro Allan Benton humbly claims it's not difficult to make; his bacon is just aged a little longer than most, 15 to 18 months on a rub of brown sugar, salt, and sodium nitrite. It famously has an extreme smokiness, owing to the intense hickory it's prepared over. Open a packet of Benton's and your neighbors can smell it. It's truly the Islay scotch of bacon. Which is why Lee initially opted for pairing it with Four Roses Yellow Label; he thought its sweet roundness and spicy rye backbone could offset the smoke.

4 TO 6 STRIPS BENTON'S HICKORY SMOKED COUNTRY BACON

ONE 750-MILLILITER BOTTLE FOUR ROSES YELLOW LABEL BOURBON

Use kitchen shears to cut the bacon strips into ¾-inch pieces. Cook over low to medium-low heat until all the fat has been released and the bacon is fully crisped. Remove the bacon and try to filter out the little bacon bits that have been left behind. (As anyone too lazy to clean the morning's bacon skillet knows, bacon fat will eventually solidify. Once it does, you can store it almost indefinitely.) Combine about $1\frac{1}{2}$ ounces warm bacon fat with the bourbon in a mixing glass or a stainless-steel container and stir until it dissolves. Allow the mixture to infuse, uncovered, at room temperature for about 4 hours, then cover and place in the freezer for 2 more hours. The fat will have risen to the top. Skim that off and strain the rest of the bourbon through a cheesecloth. You will have lost a few ounces and the yield should be about 24 ounces now. Funnel back into the bourbon bottle—explicitly relabel it—and store in the fridge.

BENTON'S OLD-FASHIONED

MAKES 1 COCKTAIL

If your bacon-infused bourbon is too smoky, consider using it for cocktails. In fact, Lee created this cocktail to add some balance. The ingredients are meant to evoke a lazy weekend morning, with maple syrup oozing across the plate and onto your bacon, it all getting washed down by some OJ.

2 OUNCES BENTON'S BACON FAT–INFUSED FOUR ROSES BOURBON (RECIPE PRECEDES)

¼ OUNCE DEEP MOUNTAIN GRADE B MAPLE SYRUP

2 DASHES ANGOSTURA BITTERS

ORANGE TWIST, FOR GARNISH

Pour the bourbon, syrup, and bitters into a mixing glass with ice and stir until chilled. Strain into a rocks glass with a giant ice cube in it. Express the orange twist over the drink and use as a garnish.

OATMEAL BOURBON

Upon opening in Dallas's Deep Ellum neighborhood in early 2016, HIDE was immediately one of the most experimental cocktail bars in the city—its prep lab employs a centrifuge and a rotovap and even cuts its ice using a frickin' laser. Luckily, you can jerry-build one of HIDE's coolest creations in the privacy of your own home. As HIDE's director of beverage and its principal bartender, Jenkins wanted to craft a cocktail that might mimic one of his childhood favorites—apple and cinnamon oatmeal. So he started with an oat-infused bourbon.

1 LITER BOURBON, PREFERABLY HIGHER PROOF WITH A HIGH-RYE PROFILE

6 OUNCES STEEL-CUT OATS

3 CINNAMON STICKS, CRACKED

Pour the bourbon into a vessel containing the steel-cut oats. Drop the cracked cinnamon sticks into the liquid. After letting the infused bourbon mixture stand for 3 hours, pour the solution through a strainer into a saucepan to remove the largest particles. Heat the solution on low, stirring frequently for 10 minutes. This will allow some of the starches from the oats to turn to sugar. Do not allow the solution to boil, as this will burn off alcohol. After the solution cools, pour through a coffee filter or other very fine-mesh strainer to remove any remaining particles.

THE TURBO QUAKER BATCH

At HIDE, Jenkins prebatches 400 milliliters of this oat-infused bourbon with 400 milliliters of cream sherry and 200 milliliters of milk-washed applejack. This is called the Turbo Quaker Batch. (Milk washing is used mainly to soften the astringency of the applejack, but it's a step you can skip at home if need be.) To milk wash, simply combine the apple jack and milk in a vessel. Allow the flavors to blend, then strain out the milk fat through a fine mesh strainer.

TURBO QUAKER

MAKES 1 COCKTAIL

If the spirituous portion of Jenkins's cocktail requires some serious advance preparation, the effort is truly worth it. The resulting libation will be velvety in texture with a comforting flavor profile despite, let's just say, an ample amount of alcohol. While the batching makes the Turbo Quaker quick to deliver in service, for the at-home mixologist it's great for utilizing at late-in-the-year cold-weather parties and gatherings.

2½ OUNCES TURBO QUAKER BATCH (RECIPE PRECEDES)

1 EGG WHITE

½ OUNCE ALMOND ORGEAT

FEE BROTHERS BLACK WALNUT BITTERS, FOR GARNISH

GRATED NUTMEG, FOR GARNISH

Pour the Turbo Quaker Batch and egg white into a shaker with ice. Shake with 6 or 7 "hard" shakes. Strain into an empty shaker half using a Hawthorne strainer. Dump the ice from the other half of the shaker. Add the Almond Orgeat and a Booker & Dax Cocktail Cube (a $20 rubber cube which improves texture). Close the container and dry shake aggressively until frothy. Pour the cocktail through a chinois into a chilled coupe glass. Garnish with a swipe of bitters and grated nutmeg.

ALEX CHIEN'S

CEREAL MILK BOURBON PUNCH

Believe it or not, a version of cereal milk whiskey dates back hundreds of years, with bottles of it even found in Charles Dickens's home, who was clearly playing with firewater well before nerds on Reddit were. Columbus, Ohio, bartender Chien, along with his Watershed Kitchen & Bar cohorts Joshua Gandee and Chris Manis, dreamed up this modern version "mostly because we wanted an excuse to return to all the cereals our moms wouldn't let us eat as children." Although making this is a tad time-consuming, it's well worth it. Take that, Mom!

3¾ CUPS SUGAR

ZEST OF 6 LEMONS

ZEST OF 2 ORANGES

¾ TEASPOON GROUND CLOVES

½ TEASPOON GROUND CARDAMOM

¾ TEASPOON GROUND ALLSPICE

½ TEASPOON GROUND CORIANDER

2 WHOLE STAR ANISE

2 PINEAPPLES—PEELED, CORED, AND CUBED

¾ CUP FRESH LEMON JUICE

45 OUNCES BOURBON

1½ TEASPOONS LOOSE-LEAF TEA (CHIEN DOES A 50/50 SPLIT OF CHAI AND YERBA MATÉ)

3 CUPS HOT WATER

½ GALLON WHOLE MILK

⅓ BOX KIDS' CEREAL—USE YOUR FAVORITE; CHIEN USES CAP'N CRUNCH

Pour the sugar into a large Cambro. Gently press the citrus zest into the sugar, creating what's called an oleo-saccharum. Combine the cloves, cardamom, allspice, coriander, and star anise in a mortar and muddle before adding to the oleo-saccharum. Muddle the pineapples into the oleo-saccharum and add the lemon juice and bourbon. Steep your tea blend in the hot water for 4 minutes and strain before adding it to your punch. Now strain out the solids, leaving an opaque punch.

Combine the milk with the cereal. If you have a vacuum sealer, vacuum-seal and rest it for 30 minutes so the milk quickly absorbs the cereal flavor. If you do not have one, simply combine in a bowl and stir occasionally as it sits for 30 minutes. Strain out the solids and pour into a large pot.

Heat up your pot of cereal milk, but do not allow it to boil. Once hot, pour into a large Cambro. Add the bourbon punch to the cereal milk, not the other way around. Leave in the refrigerator, undisturbed, for 12 to 24 hours. Gently take your Cereal Milk Bourbon Punch out of the fridge, being careful not to disturb the milk curds. Place your strainer over an empty Cambro and line it with a cheesecloth. Gently ladle your punch through the strainer. After some time you will have worked your way through to the settled milk curds, which will now be a "nest." Take your strained punch and re-strain it through the same cheesecloth. (Do not use a new cheesecloth as you need the nest of milk curds to achieve clarity.)

SATURDAY MORNING CARTOONS

MAKES 1 COCKTAIL

Essentially a fat-washed bourbon punch, Chien calls this "the best holiday treat you can give someone." You get the roundness and texture of milk in a refreshing cocktail.

1½ OUNCES CEREAL MILK BOURBON PUNCH (RECIPE PRECEDES)

1½ OUNCES SODA WATER

Pour some punch over a large ice cube in a rocks glass. Top with soda water. Go watch *Muppet Babies* without waking up your parents.

TEXAS BRISKET WHISKEY

Last time I was in Texas I think I must have eaten barbecue for every single meal, and most of the time that meant brisket. Texans love their brisket so much that one man decided to put it in his whiskey. Allan Hall is the head distiller at Ranger Creek Brewing & Distilling in San Antonio, but he's had many lives before that. Born and raised in Alaska, he eventually became a mai tai-making bartender on the Big Island in Hawaii, and his early forays into distilling involved producing chemicals for fabrication at a waste laboratory. He finally found his life's passion at his current job, telling me, "It's like owning a lemonade stand for adults."

Part of owning a lemonade stand, though, is convincing customers to buy your product. And Hall had been struggling in trying to get bartenders to use his slightly sweet, unaged white bourbon for their infusions. With the vaunted San Antonio Cocktail Conference coming to town in January of 2017, he wanted to really wow them.

"It goes back to your college days, you know, trying to create infusions. Ginger vodka and whatnot," he explains. "But I wanted to try something herbal and savory over that sweeter bubble gum-type infusion."

His first effort used beef jerky for an infusion—and the cocktail conventioneers raved. Then his friend John Herdman, the chef at Sustenio, challenged him to step it up a bit. With brisket. Lots and lots of brisket.

Several hundred dollars' worth. Released in a mere 90 bottles, and strictly to the distillery's special Texas Whiskey Club members, Brisket Whiskey was a massive hit.

"The nose is like a wet dog," Hall tells me. "It's like, 'Oh boy, that's a real fatty smell! A little bit salty, a little bit smoky.'" I asked him if it was feasible that this ever become a widely produced product. Isn't brisket expensive these days?

"Fortunately . . . we're in Texas," he noted.

4 POUNDS TEXAS BEEF BRISKET WITH FAT

2 OR 3 DRIED CHILES (ANCHOS IF YOU JUST WANT TO FLIRT WITH HEAT, CHIPOTLES IF YOU HAVE MORE BRAVADO)

1 HEAD ROASTED GARLIC, PEELED

COARSE SALT, LIKE MALDON

1 GALLON RANGER CREEK .36 WHITE (OR ANY 100-PROOF WHITE WHISKEY HEAVY ON THE CORN BILL)

Make (or buy) some prepared brisket that has been lightly seasoned. Dehydrate until there is no water remaining. If you don't have a dehydrator, simply overcook the brisket in a slow cooker. Chop the brisket and chiles into fine pieces and combine with the garlic, salt, and bourbon in a glass or stainless-steel container (at least 2-gallon), then cover. Allow the mixture to infuse in a cold area for up to two weeks, tasting along the way. When ready, place in the freezer overnight. The next day, once taken out of the freezer, immediately strain through a chinois and return to the bottle. As an alternative, for a quicker infusion, you can sous-vide (see page 188) all the ingredients together and then fat wash.

BRISKETINI

MAKES 1 COCKTAIL

While Hall thinks brisket bourbon is made to drink neat or on the rocks, others will undoubtedly want to play around with it in cocktails. If that's the case, Hall advises not doing anything sweet like an Old-Fashioned, as he claims simple syrup just turns the brisket bourbon "cringey." He thinks a Bloody (Brisket) Mary is a good option (add a flamed spear of prosciutto for garnish) for enhancing texture and presentation. But the best option is how his wife likes to drink it—as a dirty martini variant.

2 OUNCES TEXAS BRISKET WHISKEY (RECIPE PRECEDES)

½ OUNCE DRY VERMOUTH

MALDON SALT FLAKES

PICKLED CELERY STALK OR THYME SPRIG, FOR GARNISH

Pour the whiskey and vermouth into a mixing glass with ice and stir until chilled. Salt half the rim of a chilled coupe with Maldon. Strain the cocktail into the coupe and garnish with celery or thyme.

LAUREN HENCHEY'S

DELIVERY RAMEN HAKUSHU

While a student in speech pathology at the University of Vermont, Lauren Henchey also worked a side gig at Stonecutter Spirits, where she fell in love with local whiskey and also became friendly with a nearby importer of Japanese whisky. When one cold Vermont day she was sitting at home over a bowl of pork belly ramen, staring down at its fatty, oily broth, she had an idea. (If you don't dig on swine, at Jimoto Ya in Singapore, Yamazaki is fat washed with an *amaebi* [sweet shrimp] broth.)

1 ORDER TONKOTSU (PORK BELLY) RAMEN

ONE 750-MILLILITER BOTTLE HAKUSHU 12 YEAR OLD

Order delivery from the best ramen spot in your town. Eat most of the ramen, leaving a few ounces of broth and maybe some pork belly too. While still hot, combine with the Japanese whisky in a glass or stainless-steel container and stir until it dissolves. Allow the mixture to infuse, uncovered, at room temperature for 6 to 8 hours, then cover and place in the freezer for 8 more hours. The fat will have risen to the top. Skim that off and strain the rest of the bourbon through a cheesecloth. You may need to strain a second time. Funnel back into the Hakushu bottle—explicitly relabel it—and store in the fridge.

FOIE GRAS FITZGERALD

If you're going to "ruin" good whiskey, you might as well do it with the most high-end ingredient possible. Although, amusingly, when then-Boston bartender Ted Kilpatrick first made his foie gras–washed bourbon back in 2011, he used the fairly bottom-shelf Old Fitzgerald. The result was a whiskey now uniquely salty and fatty, with a hint of iron. Online whiskey geeks might claim rarity and hype is the only way to up the price of a bottle on the black market—I'd say, not so. Cramming a hundred bucks' worth of exploded duck liver into the bottle will also do the trick.

1 POUND FOIE GRAS

ONE 750-MILLILITER BOTTLE OLD FITZGERALD BOTTLED-IN-BOND

Save up your allowance and buy a pound of foie gras, assuming your municipality allows you to do so. (Close this book and move immediately if not.) Render the foie fat in a skillet over medium heat; you should get about 2 ounces of fat. Combine the warm foie fat with the bourbon in a glass or stainless-steel container and stir until it dissolves. Allow the mixture to infuse, uncovered, at room temperature for 6 to 8 hours, then cover and place in the freezer for 8 more hours. The fat will have risen to the top. Skim that off and strain the rest of the bourbon through a cheesecloth. You may need to strain a second time even. Funnel back into the bourbon bottle—explicitly relabel it—and store in the fridge. Get protested by PETA.

LA VIE DU CANARD

MAKES 1 COCKTAIL

Now the director of beverage and service at Cushman Concepts in New York, Kilpatrick came up with this cocktail while working at No. 9 Park, an elegant, James Beard Award–winning restaurant in Boston's Beacon Hill. The foie gras–washed Fitzgerald is so rich that it needed to play with some equally potent partners. The artichoke amaro Cynar brings a vegetal component, Cocchi Americano adds a sweetness and takes the aroma away from pure duck suffering, while the whiskey barrel–aged bitters do their trick and the orange peel adds needed acidity. Don't make this for your vegan buddy.

1½ OUNCES FOIE GRAS FITZGERALD (RECIPE PRECEDES)

1 OUNCE CYNAR

1 OUNCE COCCHI AMERICANO

3 DASHES FEE BROTHERS WHISKEY BARREL–AGED BITTERS

ORANGE TWIST, FOR GARNISH

Pour the Fitzgerald, Cynar, and Cocchi Americano into a mixing glass with ice, add the bitters, and stir until chilled. Strain into a rocks glass with no ice. Rub the rim with the orange twist, then use it as a garnish.

MORE FANCY AF FAT WASHES

Consider being a hoity-toity jerk and making the following as well.

A5 KOBE BEEF AND YAMAZAKI 18 YEAR OLD

The highest grade of Japanese beef almost goes down like butter. At around $150/pound, it's perfect for fat washing into a $500 bottle of sublime Japanese whisky. Of course, A5 is so "marbled" and flecked with fat, by the time you fat wash it, there might be nothing left!

ALBINO CAVIAR AND BRENNE CUVÉE SPÉCIALE FRENCH

Nicknamed "white gold," at a stunning $300,000/ kilo, Strottarga Bianca (which comes from albino sturgeon) is surely the most expensive food in the world. Fat wash it through one of the few French single malts to feel trés chic.

FRENCH PÉRIGORD BLACK TRUFFLES AND A RYE WHISKEY

This winter truffle is grown exclusively in southwestern France, only found in the wild, nestled in the roots of native oak tress. Fat wash the earthy, almost chocolately "Diamonds of Périgord" ($1000/pound) in a pre-1960s bottle of rye whiskey from southwestern Pennsylvania. Or, you can just find a bottle of Sonoma County Distilling's Black Truffle Rye, which came out in 2016 to solid reviews.

SAFFRON AND YELLOW SPOT 12 YEAR OLD

The world's most expensive spice at around $1500/lb, saffron is extremely tricky to collect en masse. Even one or two "threads" can completely change a dish, giving it a barn-like fragrance and turning everything it touches a brilliant golden-yellow color. Perfect for literally adding to Yellow Spot, a solid enough Irish whiskey.

ACORN-FED JAMÓN IBÉRICO AND NOMAD OUTLAND WHISKY

There's nothing sexier than a well-toned bare leg . . . especially when it's locked in a slicing aparatus. Spain's finest cured meat will run you about $20/ounce (or $1000 for a whole leg). Fat wash your leg in this odd ball Spanish whisky, which is distilled in Scotland, but aged in PX sherry casks in Jerez.

SOUS VIDE-SKEY

If sous vide has become the coolest way for techno-dudes to prepare their perfect steak, you can also use your immersion circulator to play with whiskey. Macerating fresh fruit or dried herbs might take weeks to work in the traditional method. Using a sous vide—like ChefSteps' Joule, which goes for under $200 these days—allows the infusion process to take just a few hours, with often better flavors being retained and minimal chance of oxidation. A particularly popular sous-vide infusion gaining steam at cocktail bars is that of bourbon and coconut flakes. To sous vide a whiskey, package the liquid alongside the food ingredients in a vacuum-sealed bag before immersing it in a water bath between 135°F and 155°F.

PEANUT BUTTER BOURBON

I've always loved the intense peanut notes in many Jim Beam products and wondered how they might be amped up by a peanut butter fat washing. Luckily, I didn't have to do any work myself as Anthony Pino of Boston's Cunard Tavern had just the technique for me. I'd like to think his recipe was created in honor of my daughter, Ellie, who has listened to Raffi's "Peanut Butter Sandwich" song so goddamn much in year two of her life that it is forever ingrained in my head.

2 CUPS PEANUT BUTTER

ONE 750-MILLILITER BOTTLE OLD GRAND-DAD BONDED

Melt the peanut butter in a saucepan over medium heat. Mix with the Old Grand-Dad Bonded. Freeze overnight. The peanut butter will sink to the bottom of the container. Skim the translucent bourbon off the top and strain the remaining mixture through coffee filters to extract the rest of the bourbon. Repeat, leaving again in the freezer overnight, then skimming and straining until the desired clarity is achieved.

Another method of peanut butter washing that has gained popularity recently, is based on a perfume-making technique called *effleurage*. You spread the peanut butter across a rimmed baking sheet, then briefly pour the bourbon over the top, before dumping it back into a serving vessel.

UNCRUSTABLE

MAKES 1 COCKTAIL

Pino's cocktail is meant to mimic the classic peanut butter and jelly sandwich. Feel free to play around with other fruit preserves.

2 OUNCES RASPBERRY GRAND CASSIS GLAZE (RECIPE BELOW)

BERRY DUST, FOR THE RIM (IN A MORTAR AND PESTLE, GRIND ½ CUP FREEZE-DRIED RASPBERRIES AND STRAWBERRIES WITH ½ CUP SUGAR)

2 OUNCES PEANUT BUTTER BOURBON (RECIPE PRECEDES)

1 OUNCE BAILEY'S IRISH CREAM

½ OUNCE FRANGELICO

Make the Raspberry Grand Cassis Glaze and coat a coup glass with a thin layer of it, then freeze it. Rim the glass with berry dust. Pour the bourbon, Bailey's, and Frangelico into a shaker with ice. Shake, then strain into the coupe.

A peanut butter sandwich made with jam, one for me and one for . . .

RASPBERRY GRAND CASSIS GLAZE
Makes about 30 ounces
2½ cups raspberry preserves
⅓ cup Lejay Cassis
1 cup Grand Marnier

Heat the raspberry preserves to just below a simmer and turn off the heat. Add the Cassis and Grand Marnier. Mix thoroughly and strain through a fine-mesh strainer to remove the seeds. Chill before using.

ROASTED NUTS JAMESON

"I would love to tell you some romanticized story about camping with a flask of whiskey and a bag of trail mix," Diego Peña, of Boston's Eastern Standard, jokes. "Truth is, I just like trail mix, and Jameson has chocolate and fruit malt notes."

1½ CUPS MIXED NUTS (PEANUTS, CASHEWS, BRAZIL NUTS, CHESTNUTS, ETC.)

1 TEASPOON SALT

1 TEASPOON SUGAR

1 TEASPOON GROUND ALLSPICE

ONE 1-LITER BOTTLE JAMESON IRISH WHISKEY

Toss the mixed nuts with the salt, sugar, and allspice and roast on a rimmed baking sheet at 350°F for about 15 minutes, until golden brown. Let cool and crush the nuts. Add to the Jameson and infuse for 24 hours in a cool place before straining. (There is no need to fat wash this whiskey for the Trail Mix Milk Punch [page 194] as the lipids bind to the milk fats at the end.)

TRAIL MIX MILK PUNCH

MAKES 3 LITERS, ABOUT 34 SERVINGS

Now I don't like camping, but I do like drinking and snacking on junk food. Therefore, I enjoy how Peña turns his Roasted Nuts Jameson into this adventurous milk punch, which is a perfect autumnal treat with its warming flavors of raisins and cacao nibs.

1 LITER ROASTED NUTS JAMESON (RECIPE PRECEDES)

17 OUNCES REHYDRATED RAISIN SYRUP (MAKE THE SYRUP BY HEATING UP EQUAL AMOUNTS OF DRIED RAISINS, WATER, AND SUGAR; LET IT COOL, PUREE IN A BLENDER, THEN STRAIN)

4 OUNCES LUSTAU AMONTILLADO SHERRY

8½ OUNCES FRESH LEMON JUICE

3 CUPS WHOLE MILK

1½ CUPS HALF-AND-HALF

1 TEASPOON CACAO NIBS

Combine the Jameson, syrup, sherry, and lemon juice in a large Cambro. Heat the milk and half-and-half with the cacao nibs in a saucepan until the mixture reaches 180°F on a candy thermometer. Add the heated milk to the punch, allowing it to rest for approximately 5 minutes before straining. Peña uses a Superbag, but you can use two chinoises lined with a single thin layer of cheesecloth to strain into two 22-quart Cambros. Once the liquid looks like it's clarifying, you can add the curds from the chinois to the batches and strain these into two new clean Cambros. A batch can take up to 12 hours to make, with constant monitoring and re-straining. Bottle the milk punch and keep refrigerated. Serve 3 ounces over ice or straight up in a dessert wine glass. Pitch a tent in your backyard and drink while telling ghost stories to your dog.

GRANDMA'S OLD GRAND-DAD

MAKES 1 COCKTAIL

As already discussed, "dusties" are one of the hottest things among whiskey collectors today. Personally, I love them. At their best, you get a rich, caramely flavor profile that has a syrupy, almost olive oil–like mouthfeel that you simply do not see in a lot of bourbons released these days. The only problem is, you pretty much can no longer find dusties because a-hole writers like me have hyped them up so much. I wondered, though . . . how could I easily re-create one? With a great play on words. Werther's Originals are the most grandma candy out there, while Old Grand-Dad is one of the most quintessential dusty finds (the bottom-shelf bottle design hasn't really changed over the decades, meaning they sometimes accidentally linger in stores).

10 PIECES WERTHER'S ORIGINAL CANDY

ONE 750-MILLILITER BOTTLE OLD GRAND-DAD BONDED

Smash the candy with a mortar and pestle and put them into the bottle. Shake hard and then store overnight. The next morning, pour through a mesh colander to capture the candies. Filter as many times as necessary. Scratch and muss up the label so the bottle looks older. Trick your friends. Get drunk and pass out. Wake up, see the bottle, and think you time-traveled backward. Shriek!

LEATHERED WHISKEY

Like Montagano's Mexican restaurant, a Houston-area German beer garden seems like an unlikely spot to see serious innovation in the whiskey world. *Falsch!* Especially when this Pearland, Texas, bar came up with the cheeky idea to make a cocktail that somehow tasted like lederhosen, the traditional leather shorts worn during Oktoberfest. While most leathers are not palatable, an all-natural calfskin—one that's been vegetable-tanned (using bark oils and veggie extracts, like what is used in baby shoes)—is completely safe and drinkable.

FOUR 750-MILLILITER BOTTLES WHISKEY (YOUR FAVORITE)

1 SQUARE FOOT VEGETABLE-TANNED LEATHER

Put the whiskey and leather in a sealable container. Start tasting after two weeks and stop when you get the flavor profile you like.

THE LEDERHOSEN SMASH

MAKES 1 COCKTAIL

While leathered whiskey might be a tad harsh and bitter on its own, adding it to a Kentucky-style smash makes it sing, finishing with just a hint of "new car" smell. Mmmmmm.

2 CUCUMBER SLICES

2 LEMON SLICES

4 TO 6 MINT SPRIGS

¾ OUNCE SIMPLE SYRUP (MAKE THE SYRUP BY HEATING UP EQUAL AMOUNTS OF WATER AND SUGAR; LET IT COOL BEFORE USING)

1½ OUNCES LEATHERED WHISKEY (RECIPE PRECEDES)

Muddle one cucumber slice, one lemon slice, and the leaves of two to four mint sprigs together in a mixing glass with the simple syrup. Add the whiskey and ice and stir until chilled. Strain into a rocks glass over ice. Garnish with any or all of the following: a fresh cucumber slice, lemon wheel, or mint sprig. Do a shoe-slapping Schuhplattler dance.

HOPPY WHISKEY

I'm likewise a craft beer fan and have enjoyed drinking along to the industry's trends over the last decade and a half. Of course, the aughts in beer were all about hops. More and more and more of them. If the 2000s were about making beers as bitter as possible, though, we're now in the era of so-called New England–style IPAs, ones made with hop varietals like Citra and Galaxy that add more juicy, tropical notes to beer.

Hops have slowly but steadily become a part of the whiskey industry too, ever since Charbay first distilled an IPA in 1999. Since then other craft distilleries like Corsair, Sons of Liberty, and Three Bines have joined in on the fun. Still, it ain't exactly easy to find a hoppy whiskey, and they aren't exactly cheap in most cases. Why not make one yourself? If you want to use a rye whiskey, opt for more piney hops like Chinook or Cascade. If you want to try a malt, opt for more floral hops like Amarillo or Centennial. Play around with combinations too.

½ OUNCE WHOLE-CONE HOPS (TRY GALAXY OR CITRA)

ONE 750-MILLILITER BOTTLE MAKER'S MARK

Load the bottom of a French press with the hops, then cover with the whiskey. After 20 minutes, plunge and pour straight back into the bottle. Infuse again if you want it hoppier.

HOP BOMBED

MAKES 1 COCKTAIL

A play on the Gold Rush that I almost called The Bold Lush.

2 OUNCES HOPPY WHISKEY (RECIPE PRECEDES)

½ OUNCE FRESH LEMON JUICE

¼ OUNCE FRESH PINEAPPLE JUICE

¾ OUNCE CLOVER HONEY SYRUP (MAKE THE SYRUP BY HEATING UP EQUAL AMOUNTS OF CLOVER, HONEY, AND WATER; LET IT COOL BEFORE STRAINING)

1 HOP CONE, FOR GARNISH

Pour all the ingredients into a shaker with ice and shake until chilled. Strain into a rocks glass over a large ice cube. Spear the hop cone and use it as a granish. Quit shaving and move to Brooklyn.

GROWN-UP SHOTS

Even if John Lermayer's cocktail bar has already found its place on the prestigious World's 50 Best Bars list, it's still located in Miami Beach, which means a lot of tourists and beachgoers enter, who often don't want anything fancier than a piña colada or strawberry daiquiri. And there's nothing wrong with that. "As a bar we like to look after everybody and their creature comforts," says Fraser Hamilton, the head bartender. "So you can have a piña colada or strawberry daiquiri here and not feel silly about it." Of course, at a world-class bar, even those drinks are going to be elevated, the former with Jamaican coffee beans and a PX sherry float, the latter with manzanilla and salt and pepper. These elevated takes also extend to two, ahem, less classy flavored whiskey shots.

FANCY FIREBALL

MAKES AROUND 45 SHOTS

The Fancy Fireball has been on the menu since opening day back in 2015, when Fireball was still red-hot (no pun) and customers were constantly asking for it. The bartenders at Sweet Liberty are not fans of flavored spirits, however, so they decided to try to make their own, higher-end version. The typical Fireball customers dug it, and even Hamilton claims, for what it's worth, "I think it tastes really good." While the bartenders at Sweet Liberty combine the ingredients to make a cocktail to order, at home you can make a larger batch to have around for your rowdier friends.

ONE 1-LITER BOTTLE OLD GRAND-DAD BONDED

1 LITER SPICED CINNAMON SYRUP (MAKE THE SYRUP BY HEATING UP EQUAL AMOUNTS OF WATER AND SUGAR, WITH 3 BROKEN CINNAMON STICKS, CLOVES, NUTMEG, AND A BAY LEAF; LET IT COOL BEFORE STRAINING)

2½ TEASPOONS SCRAPPY'S FIREWATER TINCTURE BITTERS

Combine all the ingredients in one large batch. Serve as a shot or on ice. Yell out loudly for no reason and give your bro a fist bump.

SOPHISTICATED SOCO

MAKES AROUND 16 SHOTS

SoCo was the shot of choice in, let's say, the 1970s, before Fireball was Fireball. Even by my college days in the late '90s, it was still a pretty cool thing for a young idiot to shoot. Hamilton explains that most people misunderstand that, for the longest time, Southern Comfort has essentially just been whiskey distillate and peach schnapps. (In 2017 Sazerac, the current owners of Southern Comfort, announced plans to go back to using real whiskey as an ingredient, something that hasn't been done since 1979.)

500 MILLILITERS TENNESSEE WHISKEY (JACK DANIEL'S OR GEORGE DICKEL CLASSIC NO. 8 IS FINE)

250 MILLILITERS GIFFARD CRÈME DE PÊCHE DE VIGNE

Combine the ingredients in a tiny barrel and age for a few days before bottling if you'd like, although it tastes fine without aging. Serve as a shot or on ice. Feel free to play around with infusing vanilla beans, cinnamon stick, cloves, orange peels, and even cherries into the mix. Carry the bottle around and sing "Me and Bobby McGee" in a raspy voice.

THE BLIZZARD TRIALS

When I was a kid, I used to love going to Dairy Queen and personalizing my own Blizzard. Vanilla soft serve with mashed-up candy swirled in. Was anything better? The answer is yes. Because I decided to make

some whiskey Blizzards (Whiskards?) and, as we Internet writers say, the results will amaze you. Of note, candy infuses much quicker than, ahem, *natural* ingredients. Therefore you can do these by crumbling the candy pieces into a French press or by simply  putting them directly into the bottle, shaking it, and then straining after 15 to 20 minutes. For each 10 ounces of whiskey, use 1 standard package of the following.

OREOS

Recommended whiskey: The Macallan 12 Year Old

I'm not going to lie, an Oreo infusion makes a huge mess. It will clog the filter of your French press and stick to the walls of any bottle as if the glass just became tinted. But . . . it will also taste really good. I opt for the Macallan, as the sherry barrel–finished scotch has strong chocolate notes. Oreos so overwhelm the scotch flavor, though, that you could almost certainly just use something from the bottom shelf. Even through a filter, Oreo scotch comes out quite gritty. If you have time, I recommend a fat wash to add clarity and smoothness.

BUTTERFINGER

Recommended whiskey: Booker's

I find Jim Beam's barrel-proof small-batch offering, Booker's, to have intense peanut notes. Which seemed perfect to pair with the peanut-buttery Butterfinger (singular—I bet you didn't realize that). Almost instantly the whiskey became murky and orangish. By the time it was ready to serve, it was straight confectionery. Booker's is a hot bourbon unto itself, but infused with Butterfinger it smooths out a bunch. Served over ice, it's pure decadence.

HEATH BAR

Recommended whiskey: Redbreast 12 Year Old

My typical Blizzard toss-in as a kid. I still love it today. The potent, tooth-ruinous icky sticky toffee inherent in Heath seemed a swell match for Redbreast 12 Year Old, one of my favorite Irish whiskeys. Since Heath is much sturdier and less porous than a lot of other candy bars, it's a must that you break the bar into small, almost dusty crumbles. It will eventually intensify the toffee notes and texture of the whiskey in a quite lovely way.

REESE'S PEANUT BUTTER CUP

Recommended whiskey: Knob Creek

Another Beam product, although a slightly lower-proof one, for another peanut-buttery toss-in. While this doesn't become quite as viscous as the Butterfinger Booker's, the chocolate notes of the Reese's play much better with the Knob Creek. This one is easier to drink neat, but over ice, or even in an Old-Fashioned or other typical bourbon cocktail, it would work well.

ON COLD FINGERING

I first heard the term when I least expected to. I had been searching for a way to raise the proof on certain commercial whiskeys that had a decent enough flavor profile but were far too puny in their heft and heat. "Cold fingering" was the term, and it was coming out of the mouth of Dr. Bill Lumsden as he walked me through Ardbeg's barrel warehouse. Lumsden claimed this cold fingering was the only way to raise the proof of a barrel of scotch if it had accidentally fallen below the legal 40% ABV threshold. However, he was sure to note, cold fingering was very much illegal. And therefore he didn't exactly elaborate on what cold fingering was.

I started asking other distillers about cold fingering, including Lumsden's right-hand man, Brendan McCarron. As knowledgeable as anyone in the industry, he'd never heard the term. Neither had anyone else I asked. Lumsden is a bit of a jokester, so I started to assume he had just been screwing around with me, a dumb and naive writer. Cold fingering. Ha! And then I reached out to the one man who might actually know if raising proof on commercial whiskey was truly possible, Dave Arnold.

Arnold is perhaps the world's maddest scientist of alcohol, a chef, a bar owner (formerly of the brilliant Booker & Dax), an inventor, and even an author of the unbelievable *Liquid Intelligence*. He told me he had actually used a rotary evaporator (rotovap) in the past to raise proof, which is where the term *cold fingering* might very well come from. A cold finger is a finger-shaped device used as a condenser on some rotovaps, able to cool alcohol down to a temperature of −78°C and thus eliminate water and raise proof. Still, he couldn't recommend this form of "vacuum" distillation for my purposes, calling it "a bit of a pain in the rear," not to mention something that costs many thousands of dollars.

Instead, he recommended a simple freeze concentration, or "cryo-concentration," for which you'll need a bottle of puny 80-proof whiskey and a 10-inch square block of dry ice. Pour the whiskey into an open container like a Cambro and place in a Styrofoam or plastic cooler. Place your block of dry ice in 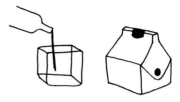 the cooler next to the open container and close the cooler. Wait until the liquor is below the crystallization point (for 80-proof whiskey this starts around −23°C). When crystals form, filter them out before they melt using a French press or a filter paper–lined funnel. The new alcohol content can be measured with a hydrometer.

CHAPTER 7

WASTING

THE MOST FUN WAYS TO DISRESPECT WHISKEY

There's a guy I know. He's not my friend, but he's a friend of some friends. At least on Facebook. He doesn't just collect and hoard all the usual suspects for his bunker; he also collects empty whiskey bottles. In fact he frequently begs people in online whiskey groups for their "empties"—the more exotic the better, so no Jack or Jim. Now, while there is indeed a rabid crime syndicate of people who buy empty bottles of Pappy and the like on eBay (not as cheap as you'd think!) and refill them with non-Pappy and the like and then illicitly sell them for secondary market prices . . . that's not what this guy is doing. Instead, he uses his empty bottles to make lamps.

Yes, lamps. Ugly, silly, ridiculous lamps that have an empty bottle of whiskey as their base. Apparently he has a decent business going, and

people pay him a good $300 for these monstrosities. What do these people do with them? I have no clue. I have good taste and a wife who I want to make sure continues to love me.

I bring this guy up because a variety of people and companies are trying to capitalize on the collective thirst for whiskey, not by creating better stuff to drink but by producing silly secondary and tertiary products loosely tied to whiskey. Publicists frequently reach out to me to try to get me to write about these silly products.

Watches made of barrel wood and bicycles from repurposed barrel heads. Whiskey barrel–aged coffee and maple syrup and even . . . blue jeans? Actually, those sounded kinda cool, and I actually wanted a pair (they were sold out).

Alas, this nonsense needs to stop. Having fun with whiskey is the point of this book. So let's actually have fun *with whiskey*. Not with its by-products. In this chapter we will look at the craziest ways to use your whiskey. The silliest ways to drink it. The most fun ways to cook with it. A way to even bathe in it. Ways that others will call a "waste"!

Until they try for themselves.

PAPPY JELL-O SHOTS

If any spot is the capital of whiskey in America, it could very well be Louisville. You stumble into any of the city's top bars—The Silver Dollar, Proof on Main—and you're absolutely awed by the selection of brown stuff. Special house single-barrel picks. Vintage whiskeys you didn't even know still existed. Limited-edition bottles you could only dream of seeing at the two-bit bars in your cruddy hometown.

In November of 2014, Meta was a fairly new spot on the Louisville scene, specializing in classic cocktails and—what else?—bourbon. And then, for the first time, it got its yearly allotment of Pappy Van Winkle. Not a lot, but enough to create a frenzy. However, instead of falling prey to the hype, instead of gouging his customers, co-owner Jeremy Johnson decided to get a little silly.

"I've lived in Kentucky since I was 10. Whiskey is friendship, community; it's about drinking it," Johnson explains, having noted how he hates that high-end bourbon became a way of boardroom-type back slapping. "And I had been saying for months: If I ever get Pappy, I'm making Jell-O shots out of it."

Yes, Johnson decided to waste his Pappy by making $10 Jell-O shots.

"The hoops we've had to jump through to get just a little bit is ridiculous," he noted at the time. "So this is a fun way to say, 'Don't forget about the other bourbons out there,' and also to celebrate Pappy time."

Still, even Johnson wasn't simply mixing Pappy 15 with a box of powdered grape gelatin. Johnson knew that Jell-O mix and bourbon didn't exactly taste all that good together. So he figured out a way to make Old-Fashioned Jell-O shots. With that stroke of genius, his local  fame became an international online viral sensation. And he became this book's Patron Saint of "wasting whiskey."

OLD-FASHIONED JELL-O SHOTS

MAKES AROUND 50 SHOTS

You can still taste the Pappy in this high-end Jell-O shot, which was completely Johnson's intention. Still, since his stunt went viral, he claims not to have heard much from Buffalo Trace, and to only rarely get its allocated products. That's fine with the ever-inventive bartender; he just started making snow cones using $200 bottles of Jim Beam Distiller's Masterpiece instead.

ONE 750-MILLILITER BOTTLE PAPPY VAN WINKLE'S FAMILY RESERVE BOURBON 15 YEAR OLD

2 OUNCES SIMPLE SYRUP (SEE PAGE 200)

15 DASHES ANGOSTURA BITTERS

2 POUCHES (ABOUT 2 TABLESPOONS) KNOX GELATIN, UNFLAVORED

1 CUP WATER

MARASCHINO CHERRIES

Using the Pappy, simple syrup, and bitters, make a large batch of Old-Fashioneds (you can tweak the above amounts to your preferred strength and flavor). In a separate bowl, stir together the gelatin and boiling water until it has fully dissolved. Combine your Old-Fashioned batch and the gelatin solution, then pour into individual plastic shot glasses that already have a maraschino cherry in them. Put in the refrigerator until solid. Pull out of the fridge. Piss people off. Party!!!

BABY GOT
PICKLEBACK

I've had a lot of bad roommates in my life. A rarely showered vegan yogi who slept on a wood slat. A messy straight-edge punk who never changed his boxers. A variety of alcoholics who would piss the bed, flip the mattress, then piss it again. Yet my worst roommate of all time was this guy Richard. Richard slept with a loaded Glock under his bed. He loudly binge-watched *30 Rock* into the wee hours of the morning. (A great show, but not when an episode you've already seen is keeping you up at 3:00 a.m.) Richard's favorite drink was the pickleback.

Now, I have nothing against the pickleback. It's perfectly fine to do one on *occasion*. But to have it as your favorite drink—not favorite shot but favorite *drink*—shows you just what kind of unhinged lunatic I was living with. Richard did picklebacks at home, he did them when he was alone, he did them on dates, he did them as he curse-cheered on his beloved New York Jets. Of course, his preferred pickleback consisted of Vlasic jar juice and "Jamo" (Jameson).

We can do better than that. Richard, this section is dedicated to you, wherever you are currently locked up.

For each of the following, do one shot of the whiskey followed by one shot of the listed pickle brine. Many of the pickle juices below can be acquired easily at your local supermarket in that section with the giant tubs of self-serve pickles and olives and stuff. Just scoop out some brine into a plastic tub. In fact, at my Whole Foods they don't even charge you for just a tub of brine (because they probably feel sorry for you).

BUSHWICK COUNTRY CLUB PICKLEBACK

Whiskey: Old Crow

Pickle Brine: McClure's Spicy Pickles

Reggie Cunningham, a bartender at the Williamsburg hipster hangout, is generally credited with inventing the "pickleback" term, if not the shot itself, back in 2006. While Old Crow is a quintessential bottom-shelf Kentucky bourbon, McClure's is a partially Brooklyn-based company with expensive-ass pickles that was, at the time, a neighbor of the bar.

BREAD AND BUTTERED UP

Whiskey: Craigellachie 13

Pickle Brine: Bread and butter

Kinda nasty on its own, the sweet and tangy bread and butter pickle works great on sandwiches and especially burgers. Meanwhile, this Speyside scotch is particularly fiery and even sulfurous, at times expressing itself with the taste of grilled ground beef. Add in a shot of liquid nacho cheese and/or ketchup to really get the alcoholic cheeseburger effect going and super-impress your friends.

HALF & HALF

Whiskey: George Dickel Rye

Pickle Brine: Half sour

Although it sounds strange, some rye whiskeys express a slight dill pickle note on the nose. This can be seen most noticeably in a few of MGP's more notably sourced ryes. Shoot the dill rye, finish with a half sour, and you're good to go.

THE KOSHER KRUSHER

Whiskey: Pikesville Straight Rye Whiskey

Pickle Brine: Kosher dill

Get a tub of those robust, super-garlicky dill pickles from your local Jewish deli. Then bang a shot of Pikesville Rye, a terrific high-proof value rye from Heaven

Hill, which, drum roll, is still owned by the Jewish Shapira family. The rye is extra spicy like a pastrami sandwich and a perfect match for the kosher pickle.

THE CRIME CAPER

Whiskey: Jefferson's Ocean Aged at Sea bourbon

Pickle Brine: Capers

Little ball bearings of explosive saltiness, the caper is quite divisive. I love them, though, especially paired with smoked salmon on my morning bagel. A much-mocked dram among the cognoscenti, Jefferson's Ocean is, well, literally aged in barrels aboard a boat at sea. The gimmicky offering nevertheless has wonderfully briny, savory notes, like a slab of lox. All that's missing now is a schmear.

SALT-N-PEPPADEW

Whiskey: Caol Ila 12 Year Old

Pickle Brine: Peppadew

If you ask me, the most underrated serve-yourself pickle at the grocers is the peppadew, those juicy sweet and tangy orange-red balls. Pairing them with a drier, saltier dram like Caol Ila (an Islay distillery near the Sound of Islay) is perfect.

BEETS BY JURA

Whiskey: Isle of Jura "Origin" 10 Year Old

Pickle Brine: Beets

Pickled beets have a wonderful earthy flavor. Pair with Jura, a scotch that also definitely feels very much "from the land." Caveat emptor: when your urine is red in the morning, don't worry, thinking your liver has finally exploded.

SO CORNY

Whiskey: Mellow Corn

Pickle Brine: Rick's Picks Smokra

One of my unexpectedly favorite picklings is that of okra, especially this Brooklyn company's zesty one, which is spiced with Spanish smoked paprika.

Okra reminds me of southern food and cornbread, and this briefly aged corn whiskey works as a nice analogue. Do this pickleback with greasy hands right in the middle of a massive fried chicken meal.

THE GINGER HAMMER

Whiskey: Ohishi Whisky

Pickle Brine: Ginger

A palate cleanser of pink pickled ginger is a must at sushi spots. And it ain't sushi without rice. Amazingly, there are some fine Japanese rice whiskies that have recently been released. (Yes, I know some people consider rice whisky to be *shōchū*.) Look for the brandy or sherry cask version of Ohishi if you really want to get tossed out of the fancy omakase restaurant where you're pulling off this stunt.

LI'L SHOT OF KIMCHI

Whiskey: Hwayo 41

Pickle Brine: Kimchi

Soju isn't really whiskey, but it kinda is, and it's the best-selling spirit in the world too. This Korean rice whiskey is meant to be served with food. Well, kimchi is food. It's like, the best food, my neighbors who shop at the local co-op tell me. Take a shot, slurp the kimchi juice. Very healthy!

SHRIMP

Whiskey: Elijah Craig Small Batch

Pickle Brine: Shrimp

And now you've just downed pickled shrimp juice after pounding whiskey . . . and it might be time to call it a night and retire your pickleback game.

PAPPY VAN VINEGAR

If for any reason, *the* reason a whiskey connoisseur is on social media is to display his collection and drinking prowess like a total a-hole. And while plenty of Instagrammers have shown a unique ability to flex their muscles by 'Gramming rare bottles they are *in media* drinking, the biggest flex I've ever seen surely belongs to Sean Brock. The famed James Beard Award–winning chef-owner of Husk and McCrady's was at one time known as a top collector of old Stitzel-Weller bourbons. Although he no longer drinks, Brock still is able to blow away the whiskey geeks. As he did in the summer of 2017, when he posted a picture of a tiny squeeze bottle, a hand-printed label on it simply reading "23 Yr. Pappy Dried Oyster Vinegar."

Of course, his followers were sent into a tizzy. "Mind blown," "You are my idol!!!," and "Whaaaaaaaaa?????" were some of the comments.

A self-proclaimed vinegar obsessive, Brock has long been known for making vinegars out of curious things like Pabst Blue Ribbon and Mountain Dew. Using Pappy Van Winkle 23 Year Old was his most audacious move yet. As with Meta's Jeremy Johnson, this was wasting whiskey par excellence.

Even more so than Johnson, though, as Brock had literally turned America's most coveted alcohol . . . nonalcoholic.

BOURBON VINEGAR

MAKES 1 QUART

You'll never quite be able to make Brock's vinegar, as he uses a decades-old vinegar starter he inherited from his grandma when she died. For average schmoes like us who don't have vinegar-obsessed grandmothers, he recommends using a store-bought "cheater" as your starter.

This recipe calls for almost a full bottle of Pappy, but it will leave you with one ounce you can actually drink!

24 OUNCES PAPPY VAN WINKLE'S FAMILY RESERVE BOURBON 23 YEAR OLD

8 OUNCES BRAGG ORGANIC RAW UNFILTERED APPLE CIDER VINEGAR

Mix the bourbon and cider vinegar together in a large container. Cover tightly with 5 layers of cheesecloth rubber-banded around the top and store in a cool, dark corner for at least a month. (Storing it in too warm a spot may attract fruit flies.) The longer stored, the greater the potential depth of flavor. Keep 1 cup of the vinegar to use as the starter for your next batch, which will taste even better. Store the rest in squeeze bottles labeled "23 Yr. Pappy Vinegar." Post on Instagram to brag.

JASON ROWAN'S

WHISKEY BITTERS

An integral part of most all whiskey cocktails, bitters add balance, draw out the flavors of your other ingredients, and add complexity. Unfortunately, most everyone is still stuck using the basic Angostura or Peychaud's sold at the supermarket. While those are undoubtedly great, why not make some yourself? Even better, if most bitters use a base of neutral grain spirit, what if you used a whiskey base for even more flavor?

Jason Rowan is a friend and a fellow spirits writer, most regularly for *T: The New York Times Style Magazine.* He's likewise a bitters expert who cofounded Brooklyn Hemispherical Bitters. While homemade bitters typically call for a vodka or grain alcohol base, this is Rowan's favorite bourbon-based bitters recipe.

24 OUNCES OLD GRAND-DAD 114 (OR ANOTHER HIGH-PROOF BOURBON)

1 TABLESPOON BURDOCK ROOT

½ TABLESPOON GENTIAN ROOT

1 TEASPOON DANDELION ROOT

1 TEASPOON CORIANDER SEEDS

½ TEASPOON CARDAMOM PODS

1 STAR ANISE

¾ TEASPOON WILD CHERRY BARK

1 CINNAMON STICK

1 VANILLA BEAN, SEEDS REMOVED

¼ CUP DRIED ORANGE PEEL

12 OUNCES WATER

In a Cambro, mix together all the ingredients except the water, stirring for a few minutes. Over the next three days, continue stirring several times a day. On the fourth day, add the water. Then continue stirring a few times a day for the next 19 days. As you near the three-week mark, start tasting the mixture. It will have a perfumy taste initially, but when it reaches its optimum "bitterness" you'll know it's done, as that floral fragrance and taste will dissipate and the elements will coalesce into the delicious bitters taste you are familiar with. (Note: If you want it more citrusy and sweet, use more orange peel and cardamom. If you want it more bitter, bump up the burdock and gentian.)

ACTING CORDIAL

MAKES AROUND 24 OUNCES

You can likewise use your newfound skills of maceration to make a cordial—in this case a whiskey one that will work swell during the holiday season.

ONE 750-MILLILITER BOTTLE MAKER'S MARK

1 CUP DRIED CHERRIES, HALVED

5 DATES, HALVED

2 DRIED PLUMS, HALVED

1 CINNAMON STICK

1 VANILLA BEAN

Combine all the ingredients in a mason jar and cover. Set aside in a cool, dark place for 4 months, shaking occasionally. At that point, begin tasting until the desired flavor profile is reached. Strain through a chinois, then blend or juice the fruits along with the whiskey, and bottle. Give as gifts or chug the whole thing at your office Christmas party.

WHISKEY NIP GAME HEN

One of the more visually stunning backyard barbecue dishes is the infamous beer can chicken. A chicken is stood upright with a can of Bud shoved up its tush, and the heat causes the beer's vapors to rise, which flavor and moisten the meat. Well, this book is about whiskey, not beer, so I decided to see if I could make a whiskey butt chicken. Of course, I ain't gonna shove a solid glass bottle of booze up my bird. Instead, I thought, why not use those tiny, 50-milliliter "nips" favored by airlines and secret alcoholics?

(Some people will dispute whether making the so-called "drunken" bird actually works. The way I see it, the boiling point of beer is above 212°F, the boiling point of pure alcohol is 173°F, and whiskey is thus somewhere in between. And, okay, even if it doesn't work flavor-wise, damn, does it look cool.)

1 GAME HEN

OLIVE OIL

BOURBON SALT RUB (RECIPE FOLLOWS)

3 "NIPS" BOURBON (PLASTIC BOTTLES ONLY)

BOURBON SPRAY (RECIPE FOLLOWS)

Remove the fat and other junk from the bird's cavity. Dry with paper towels, coat in olive oil, and cover both the inside and outside with the

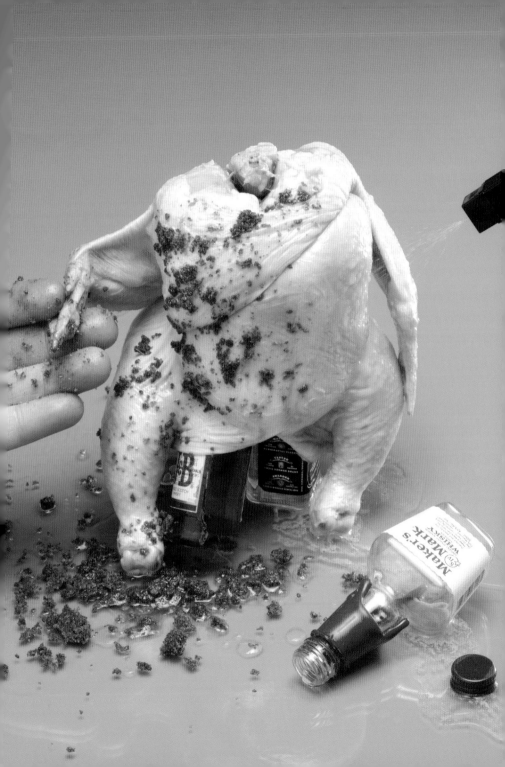

bourbon salt rub. You have two options next: the easy way or the visually stunning, grab-all-those-Instagram-likes way. The easy way is to take an empty beer can, make two additional holes on the top, and then pour the whiskey nips into that. The cooler way is to simply crack the tops on the three nips and jam them up the hen's behind in a tripod formation.

Prepare a medium-high heat grill or smoker using wood you've doused in the same bourbon. Place the hen over indirect heat, standing on their beer can or nip tripod, above a drip pan. Cook for a little over 1 hour, until nicely browned and cooked through (about 180°F; yes, more than is needed to boil alcohol!), basting every 15 minutes with the bourbon spray. Let the hen rest for 5 minutes, take a dope picture of it, then carefully lift it off the can or nips tripod, being careful not to spill the hot whiskey on yourself. Carve and serve, periodically checking all the Instagram likes you've been racking up.

You're an #influencer now, baby!

BOURBON SALT RUB

Makes 1 cup

¾ cups bourbon

¼ cup sea salt

¼ cup dark brown sugar

¼ cup cayenne

¼ cup ground cumin

In a small saucepan, boil the bourbon until reduced to 1 ounce or so, then use it to coat the sea salt. Spread the salt on a cookie sheet and bake at 170°F for 1 hour, mixing the salt around every 15 minutes until the bourbon has fully evaporated. Mix the bourbon salt with the brown sugar, cayenne, and cumin.

BOURBON SPRAY

Makes 1½ cups

½ cup bourbon

½ cup water

1 cup apple cider

Combine all the ingredients in a saucepan. Bring to boil, cool, and add to a spray bottle or mister.

SINGLE-MALT LOX

As a Jew, I've always liked lox on my bagels, but, hmmm, they're never quite scotchy enough now, are they? Chef Mark Hennessey has a solution for my problem and a great way to improve all our weekend mornings. Born on Long Island to an Italian mother and an Irish father ("My mother taught me how to pick out tomatoes; my father taught me how to pick out whiskey," he cracks), his life changed when he got a gig preparing kosher food. Now he's the executive chef at Le Marais, New York's first kosher steakhouse, with meat aged in the French brasserie fashion. To combine his growing ethnicities, here's how Hennessey makes a traditional Jewish lox . . . with a whiskey twist.

ONE 1½- TO 2-POUNDS SALMON FILLET

2 TO 4 OUNCES WHISKEY (FOR A SWEETER LOX, USE BOURBON. CHEF HENNESSEY PREFERS JEFFERSON'S RESERVE, BASIL HAYDEN'S, OR HUDSON BABY BOURBON. FOR A SMOKIER SALMON WITHOUT SMOKING, HE USES AN ISLAY SCOTCH LIKE ARDBEG KELPIE.)

1 CUP SALT

1 CUP SUGAR

FRESHLY GROUND BLACK PEPPER

2 TABLESPOONS FRESH LEMON JUICE

2 TABLESPOONS FRESH LIME JUICE

Pluck out the salmon's rib bones with a fish tweezer—these small tubes where the bones used to be are going to be the exact places where the fish will absorb the whiskey. Next, use a light silicone brush so it

doesn't tear the flesh, and coat both sides of the salmon with whiskey. Cover the salmon on both sides with an equal blend of salt and sugar (use brown sugar and sea salt if you plan on smoking the salmon afterward). Add black pepper to taste. Next, coat with a combination of lemon and lime juice. Place the lox in a vacuum-sealed bag or wrap in plastic as tightly as possible. Leave tightly wrapped/vacuum-sealed in the refrigerator for three or four days. Afterward, make sure to blot off all the sugar and salt, even running the salmon under cold water until it is clean. Dry and let sit uncovered on butcher paper in the dry environment of the refrigerator for a few hours before eating.

SMOKED WHISKEY SALMON

You can additionally try to cold smoke the salmon.

First, do everything in the preceding recipe, then use a cold-smoking procedure. Fill an aluminum tray with ice. Put a wire rack on top of the tray with your cured salmon on that. Put everything in a smoker for 6 to 8 hours. Take it out when the salmon is leathery and bronzed. Wrap in butcher paper to blot out more moisture and then leave in the refrigerator for 4 hours before serving. You can also try smoking with the Smoking Gun Pro.

For the most boss move of them all, take a portion of your cured and smoked salmon and fat wash it back into the same whiskey you just cured it with. Salmon single malt!

WHISKEY-AGED STEAK

It seems self-evident, but it took 'til around, oh, 2008 or so for American chefs to realize bacon makes everything taste better. Enter bacon-tasting flights, bacon-made serving vessels, bacony desserts, and lardon-laced salads galore. It's taken even longer for chefs to realize that whiskey *truly* makes everything taste better. One chef well ahead of the curve was Angie Mar. In the fall of 2016 she purchased the Beatrice Inn in New York's West Village from famed magazine editor Graydon Carter. When it reopened, her debut menu listed a total game changer: whiskey-aged steak.

Mar learned the technique from her mentor, the avant-garde Parisian butcher Yves-Marie Le Bourdonnec. While dry-aging beef is quite common, if not expected at higher-end steakhouses these days, dry-aging something wrapped in something wet is quite unusual. ("Wet-aging" beef would mean keeping it literally submerged in liquid the entire aging time.) Dry-aging beef is a timely and costly, although awesomely delicious, procedure—around 30% of the meat's moisture disappears, as the enzymes soften it while also causing amino acids to form, giving it a more complex, umami-packed, even funky flavor.

Whiskey aging adds even more flavor notes, while retaining some of the liquid that is typically lost through pure dry aging. Mar's meat takes on the sweeter notes of the Jack Daniel's she prefers to use, adding vanilla and caramely flavors unexpected in a steak. With the dreaded "$MP" in the price column on the menu, though, this uber-luxury item might be cheaper to make at home.

If you have the chutzpah.

THE NIKKA LAMB

Mar's mentor, Yves-Marie Le Bourdonnec, makes a Nikka Pure Malt "Black" whisky–injected leg of lamb. He continually injects the muscles in the animal's gigots (legs) with a hypodermic needle full of Nikka infused with juniper berries, rosemary, thyme, and pink peppercorns. (Americans might need to use Nikka Coffey Grain Whisky.) He stores it in his cold room, wrapped in a towel, but you can just use a dorm room mini-fridge. Each day for three weeks, unwrap the lamb, then inject each of the 13 muscles with a little whisky. After three weeks, roast the lamb for 36 hours at 150°F in a vacuum-sealed bag. The result will be something sweet from the Japanese whisky yet gamy from the dry aging.

JACK DANIEL'S – AGED RIB STEAKS

MAKES 5 TO 6 STEAKS

While Mar has found this "works" in as few as 125 days, and while she'd prefer to push for around 200, her menued steak usually resides at 160 days of whiskey aging.

ONE 750-MILLILITER BOTTLE JACK DANIEL'S

1 UNTRIMMED BONE-IN RIB ROAST (AVOID INDIVIDUAL STEAKS IF POSSIBLE)

Saturate several layers of cheesecloth or a towel with the whiskey, then wrap around your roast. Store on an elevated wire rack above a drip tray in a dedicated dry-aging refrigerator at 40°F (that tiny beer fridge from your dorm room will work fine). If possible, place a tiny fan inside the fridge to promote drying. You will probably need only 40 to 60 days of aging and perhaps as few as 20 to 30, depending on how much funk you like. Turn every so often to get even aging, but don't open the fridge more than once a week, as the meat will pick up outside odors. Once the cheesecloth has been removed, you will notice the steak will have changed colors and maybe even developed mold. Trim away the exterior, then cut into individual steaks. Use your preferred cooking method. You should now get whiskey flavor without any whiskey bite. If you're really adventurous, Mar pairs her steak with lobster butter and Australian winter truffles, but, come on, you're not made of money.

THE BONE
MARROW LUGE

Even if the pickleback is kinda cool, I think we can all agree that more typical shots are stupid. Yes, drinking heavily is awesome, but shots are generally for a species of people who use "Woooooooooo!" as their preferred mating call. But what if you could do a classier, more flavorful, oh-so-ostentatious shot that would look great on Instagram and have everyone in a fine restaurant thinking "I want to be that person"?

Enter the bone marrow luge.

Bone marrow used to be something poor people ate. Sorry, but facts are facts. People would cook discarded bones until the marrow portion softened and then have a high-fat, high-protein nosh. Yes, poor people usually know what tastes delicious. As with many reappropriated "peasant" dishes, it eventually started appearing as a $20 appetizer on fancy restaurant menus, usually served with a side of toast points. It's effing delicious, quite frankly. Tastes like meat butter, everyone says.

Then some wise guy noticed the inside of a scooped-out bone looks like a flume slide at the local waterpark and, well, you could probably pour some alcohol down that and directly into someone's face.

I did my first bone marrow luge at Proof on Main in Louisville, one of the country's best hotel bars, with plenty of terrific whiskey options. We used Michter's 10 as I recall. I think I charged it to a buddy's room. It was obviously spectacular.

I've never really heard of anyone doing a bone marrow luge at

home. It's more the kind of thing where you're out with the boys or some clients, and you're a little drunk, and you got an expense account, and there aren't really many people left in the restaurant, and you just decide to get stupid. But, you know, I suppose you could do one at home too.

This sherry-topped shot is inspired by a friendly waiter at Denver's Acorn. I was explaining the concept of the bone marrow luge to my brother-in-law, and he became psyched to try one. When we ordered from our waiter, another waiter butted in and recommended we do his sherry-topped blend. A self-taught sommelier of the luge, this waiter claimed, after much testing, that he found this rye-sherry marriage to be the best to luge down the fatty slide of the beef bone. I have to say, I agree with him. Unfortunately, I was pretty drunk by that point— you always are when you pull out the luge—and I never got his name. Hopefully I can credit his genius in a future edition of this book, after it wins a James Beard Award.

1 BEEF BONE, HALVED

1½ OUNCES WILD TURKEY 101 RYE, TOPPED WITH A SPLASH OF SHERRY

SALT

CHOPPED PARSLEY (OPTIONAL)

If you're lucky, a friendly butcher may give you a bone for free. Cut (or preferably have your highly skilled butcher cut) the bones the long way (because you probably don't own a band saw). Salt heavily, then bake for 20 minutes at 425°F. Remove from the oven and sprinkle with finely chopped parsley if you're fancy. Use a tiny baby doll spoon to scoop the marrow onto the best bread you own, toasted. Great, now that you have an empty bone and raised cholesterol levels, pour yourself a shot of sherry-topped whiskey. You can carefully dump that shot down the bone, which should be tilted at, oh, a 45-degree angle, into your mouth. Or you can just pour a bottle straight down the luge 'til you can't handle it anymore.

WILL IT LUGE?

My bro and fellow writer David Covucci and I developed an obsession with bone marrow luges during the summer of 2016. It evolved into a mission of finding other things that would work as an alcohol luge.

A few favorites:
- Wild Turkey from a dirty gravy boat.
- Bruichladdich scotch off discarded oyster shells.
- Jamaican rum through a fish bone carcass.
- Michter's Celebration Sour Mash from the skulls of our enemies.
- Knob Creek down celery stalks (healthy!).

WHISKEY CREAMING

MAKES AROUND 36 OUNCES

My wife is often torn about whether to end her evening with dessert or a nightcap. Why not both? While Americans mostly know whiskey cream as that of the Bailey's Irish how-does-that-not-need-refrigeration??! variety, there are quite a few other products on the market that do employ real dairy. Even those still taste a tad artificial, surely for shelf stability. Why not just make your own? It's simple, and at least you'll know what's in it. The following recipe is highly tweakable, allowing you to opt for Irish whiskey or bourbon or, hell, scotch, or to toss in additions of chocolate, coffee, or whatever you desire.

18 OUNCES WHISKEY OF CHOICE

14 OUNCES SWEETENED CONDENSED MILK

4 OUNCES HEAVY CREAM

1 TABLESPOON MELTED DARK CHOCOLATE

1 TABLESPOON VANILLA EXTRACT

1 TABLESPOON ALMOND EXTRACT (OPTIONAL)

1 TABLESPOON FINELY GROUND ESPRESSO BEANS (OPTIONAL)

Place all the ingredients together in a blender. Blend, pour into a bottle, and store in the refrigerator.

BOURBON CREAMSICLE

MAKES AROUND 36 OUNCES

For a more orangey tint to your cream, try the following recipe.

14 OUNCES SWEETENED CONDENSED MILK

4 OUNCES HEAVY CREAM

2 TABLESPOONS GRATED TANGELO ZEST

2 TABLESPOONS GRATED ORANGE ZEST

18 OUNCES BOURBON

½ OUNCE VANILLA EXTRACT

Heat the condensed milk, heavy cream, tangelo and orange zests, and stir until combined. Place in a blender with the bourbon and vanilla extract. Blend, pour into a bottle, and store in the refrigerator.

WHISKEY SOAP

You've already learned every which way to drink, eat, and consume whiskey. But maybe you love whiskey so much that you also want to bathe in it.

In 2010, at the height of the recession, despite holding a great marketing job at PepsiCo, Sam Swartz felt a need to scratch his entrepreneurial itch. He also wanted to create a product that targeted men (a group he felt had been woefully ignored by PepsiCo). He realized the soap industry might be perfect, as most bath companies marketed only to women or, in the case of Axe and Old Spice, "horny teenage boys" (his words). He furthermore wanted to speak to them like his grandfather might—with no BS.

That's why Swartz created Duke Cannon Supply Co. Their first product was going to be called Kirk Cockwood's Big Ass Brick of Soap, until an investor wisely advised him to drop the porn star name. Now simply known as the Big Ass Brick of Soap, its large shape was based on the actual soap GIs were issued during the Vietnam War. Soon Swartz was producing a soap made with Old Milwaukee Beer, a particularly big hit. He thought making a whiskey soap might be his next great idea.

"We didn't want people to smell like drunks, though," he jokes, one reason Buffalo Trace bourbon accounts for only around 1% of the soap's composition. "You walk into a bourbon rackhouse, and it really is just the best-smelling place. You have the sweetness of the bourbon fumes, the woodiness of the oak, and the 200-year-old building's unique odor."

Sounds better than Irish Spring!

While Duke Cannon Big American Bourbon Soap ("Oak Barrel Scent") is hardly an unaffordable luxury at around $10 a bar, DIYers who want to try to make their own whiskey soap will find it's easier than they'd think. Swartz gets Duke Cannon's soaps made at a giant factory in Memphis, but for home soap chefs without their own extruders and industrial-size mixers, another method will need to be followed. And, yes, for all of us who have seen *Fight Club*, we will be using fat—in this case beef tallow, the stuff that used to make McDonald's french fries taste good before they wimped out and switched to vegetable oil.

WARNING: As lye is caustic, please use gloves, long sleeves, and eye protection, glass or Pyrex measurers, and a well-ventilated work area. And please don't drink too much whiskey before attempting this craziness.

Measurements by weight, not volume:

50 OUNCES BEEF TALLOW

7 OUNCES 100% PURE LYE

18 OUNCES DISTILLED WATER

CORN KERNEL MEAL (OPTIONAL)

½ OUNCE BUFFALO TRACE BOURBON

Slowly melt the beef tallow in a pot or slow cooker that you got for your wedding but never use. Carefully stir the lye into the measured water in that order (adding water to lye can be dangerous). Stir the water lye mixture until dissolved, which will cause the water to become quite hot. Slowly stir the mixture into the melted tallow in the pot. Use an immersion blender on low speed for a better blend. Once the blend has reached a goopy, emulsified consistency (called "trace"), you can also sprinkle the corn into the mix. Bourbon is obviously made of corn, and these bits of corn act as an exfoliant, although Swartz admits they can be a tad harsh on the skin if overused. Put the lid on the pot and cook on "low" for an hour, making sure it never bubbles over.

After an hour, the mixture should look and feel soapy. Turn off the pot and allow to cool briefly. Quickly mix in the bourbon, making sure the soap doesn't set. Pour the bourbon soap mixture into molds. Silicone ice cube trays work well. Set aside overnight to allow to set fully. Pop out the soap cubes the next morning. The soap can be used immediately, although it will feel better after one or two weeks. Eating it will not get you drunk, although I can't say I've tested that fully.

Be sure to clean anything the lye has touched by soaking it in a mixture of hot, soapy water and vinegar.

YOUR HUMBLE AUTHOR'S

BOURBON BATH & BEYOND

But maybe simply using bourbon soap isn't enough to fully immerse you in the whiskey you love. Maybe you, like, literally want to be immersed, to bathe in the water of life. Surprisingly enough, that's not quite as strange as it sounds. There's actually quite a history of people bathing in alcohol, dating back as far as the Middle Ages. Even today, in pilsner-mad Prague, beer spas remain all the rage, with guests taking relaxing dips in bubbling tubs of barley, hops, and yeast. (Of course they're allowed to drink from bathside beer taps while they do it.) In Japan there are sake spas. Wine baths are a thing as well—they snootily call it "vinotherapy"— with many people believing they moisturize and revitalize skin. Former NBA star Amar'e Stoudemire liked to take postgame red wine baths, thinking it helped his circulation, although his career was shortened by chronic injuries, so who knows? Alas, there's no licensed spa, so far as I can tell, that offers a bourbon bath. It's finally time to use your fancy guest bathroom for something fun.

120 BOTTLES OF YOUR FAVORITE WHISKEY

Pour all into a bathtub and . . .

Just kidding!

If the fumes didn't quickly overtake you, the ethanol would soon go through your pores, perhaps killing you of alcohol poisoning. But what a way to go! If you insist on bathing in bourbon, try a much smaller dose, like a single bottle, mostly cut with warm water. Will it do anything for your skin or health? Probably not. But who else do you know who could say he wasted an entire bottle of bourbon on a bath? Which is kind of the point of this book in the first place.

So why not try it? I already have.

THANKS!

. . . to Nick Fauchald for coaxing me into writing this book. I never had any plans to write a whiskey book. I'm glad I took that first meeting with him. Thanks to the rest of the Dovetail team—my editor, Mura Dominko, Carlo Mantuano, the beautifully insane photo, design, and illustration work from Scott Gordon Bleicher, Justin Fuller, and Carolyn Håkansson, and, of course, Eric Prum and Josh Williams along with many others. This book is a spin-off of ideas and stories I first wrote about for PUNCH, in my opinion the best drinks website on Earth. Thus, a massive thanks to Talia Baiocchi, my editor there and a great friend, who gave me her blessing to explore these topics further in print. Thanks to the other gals at PUNCH too; it's always a highlight of my week to visit the office and prevent them from getting any work done while I drink through their latest booze samples. Thanks to all my friends and editors at the many other publications where I also have written about whiskey, most notably *Esquire*, *First We Feast*, and *Whisky Advocate*. Thanks to my wife, Betsy, for letting me have a silly job and devote a significant portion of our tiny apartment to bottles ("But why do you need so many of that same bourbon?" "They're not the same. They're all different *batches*."). Thanks to my daughter, Ellie (and my cat, Hops), for never pulling off/knocking over/breaking any bottles on the shelves. Thanks to my friend Derek, with whom I have done the vast majority of my highest-end whiskey dramming in life, often on his generous dime. Thanks to my bro David Covucci for helping me answer life's most pressing question: "Will it luge?" Thanks to Natalie Compton for introducing me to Mountian Dew mouth (may it be in the *Oxford English Dictionary* soon). Thanks to Jason Rowan for always commiserating with me about the most annoying people on Instagram. Thanks to Justin Kennedy because he thanked me in his last book and if I didn't thank him here I'd look like a dick (he is a great friend, alcohol writer, and drinking buddy too). Thanks to Postmark Cafe in Park Slope, Brooklyn, where I wrote the vast majority of this book (sober but filled with quadruple Americanos). Thanks to all the whiskey fans on the Internet who have shared their stories with me, many of whom have also become friends and whiskey consiglieres, most notably Blake Riber and David Jennings. Thanks to my fellow friends and freelance writers on the alcohol beat. I will see you soon at the next event. (Also please write about my book in a highly viral, listicle form. And don't take less than $200 for the story. You're worth it.) Finally, thanks to all the great whiskey producers across the universe, without whom I'd probably be writing books about hacking cupcake-flavored vodka. Yuck.

RESOURCES

SOME FAVORITE PLACES TO SHOP FOR WHISKEY

Astor Wine & Spirits (New York, NY) — astorwines.com

Binny's Beverage Depot (throughout the Chicago, IL, area) — binnys.com

Julio's Liquors (Westborough, MA) — juliosliquors.com

Justins' House of Bourbon (Lexington, KY) — thehouseofbourbon.com

K&L Wine Merchants (throughout CA) — klwines.com

New Hampshire Liquor & Wine Outlet (throughout NH) — liquorandwineoutlets.com

SOME FAVORITE BARS FOR DRINKING WHISKEY

Al's Wine & Whiskey Lounge (Syracuse, NY) — alswineandwhiskey.com

Belle's Cocktail House (Lexington, KY) — bellesbar.com

Bluegrass Tavern (Lexington, KY) — thebluegrasstavern.com

Caledonia (New York, NY) — caledoniabar.com

Canon: Whiskey and Bitters Emporium (Seattle, WA) — canonseattle.com

Copper & Oak (New York, NY) — copperandoak.com

Fine & Rare (New York, NY) — fineandrare.nyc

Hard Water (San Francisco, CA) — hardwaterbar.com

Jack Rose Dining Saloon (Washington, DC) — jackrosediningsaloon.com

Mordecai (Chicago, IL) — mordecaichicago.com

OBC Kitchen (Lexington, KY) — obckitchen.com

Proof on Main (Louisville, KY) — proofonmain.com

Reserve 101 (Houston, TX) — reserve101.com

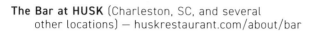

The Bar at HUSK (Charleston, SC, and several other locations) — huskrestaurant.com/about/bar

The Highland Stillhouse (Portland, OR) — highlandstillhouse.com

The Milk Room (Chicago, IL) — chicagoathletichotel.com/restaurants/milk-room

The Office (Chicago, IL, and New York, NY) — exploretock.com/theoffice

The Silver Dollar (Louisville, KY) — whiskeybythedrink.com

WHERE TO BUY HARD-TO-FIND INGREDIENTS

Dandelion Botanical Company (Seattle, WA) — dandelionbotanical.com

Kalustyan's (New York, NY) — foodsofnations.com

Starwest Botanicals (Sacramento, CA) — starwest-botanicals.com

TIC Gums (White Marsh, MD) — ticgums.com

CONTACT INFORMATION FOR DISTILLERIES OFFERING SINGLE BARREL "PICKS"

Barrell Bourbon — orders@barrellbourbon.com

Dad's Hat Pennsylvania Rye — info@DadsHatRye.com

Four Roses Bourbon — Mandy Vance, mvance@fourrosesbourbon.com

High West Distillery — Justin Lew, justin.l@highwest.com

Jack Daniel's — 888-551-5225

Jim Beam — singlebarrel@beamsuntory.com

Maker's Mark — singlebarrel@beamsuntory.com

Old Forester — old_forester@pobox.oldforester.com

Sazerac — Beau Beckman, bbeckman@sazerac.com

WhistlePig — Gregory Gatti, gregory@whistlepigrye.com

Wild Turkey — Katrina Egbert, katrina.egbert@campari.com,
502-839-2176

Woodford Reserve — woodford_reserve@pobox.woodfordreserve.com

Wyoming Whiskey — Frank Sacca, frank@wyomingwhiskey.com

ABOUT THE AUTHOR

© CORY SMITH

Aaron Goldfarb is a novelist and the author of *How to Fail: The Self-Hurt Guide*, *The Guide for a Single Man*, and *The Guide for a Single Woman*. He writes about whiskey for *Esquire*, PUNCH, and *Whisky Advocate*. This is his first book on the subject. He lives in Park Slope, Brooklyn, with his wife, Betsy; daughter, Ellie; and Maine Coon cat, Hops.

INDEX

Page numbers in *italics* indicate illustrations or photos